LINGERING CHARM OF *Delhi* MYTH, LORE AND HISTORY

R.V. SMITH

PAPER MISSILE
NIYOGI BOOKS

Published by
NIYOGI BOOKS
Block D, Building No. 77,
Okhla Industrial Area, Phase-I,
New Delhi-110 020, INDIA
Tel: 91-11-26816301, 26818960
Email: niyogibooks@gmail.com
Website: www.niyogibooksindia.com

Editor: Jayalakshmi Sengupta
Design: PealiDezine

ISBN: 978-93-85285-18-9
Year of Publication: 2016
Reprint: 2018

Printed at: Niyogi Offset Pvt. Ltd., New Delhi, India

Dedicated to Zakir Husain Delhi College, the only surviving educational institution of Mughal days, which has thrived under a galaxy of principals, whose successor, Dr M. Aslam Parvaiz continues to maintain the age-old tradition of this renamed portal of learning.

Contents

NOSTALGIC MEDLEY

FOREWORD

R.V. Smith has been writing delightful articles in the *Hindu* and the *Statesman* for years—in the latter newspaper continuously, for half a century. The repertoire is so wide that it attracts the attention of even people who are in the habit of just flipping through the morning papers. A virtual feast of heady topics is laid before the reader who willy-nilly gets engrossed in it. Sample the stuff offered in this selection—romance, mysticism, history, music, nostalgic tales, great personalities and occult happenings.

The aura of the Raj days gives an idea to the younger generation of the events that fascinated their forefathers. World War memories are brought alive too as one reads about Noor Inayat Khan who spied for the Allied forces and met her end at the hand of Nazi soldiers in Germany. Among other outstanding personalities are Hakim Ajmal Khan and also Dr Sen, the early 20th century doctor of Chandni Chowk, hailed as a messiah when medicine had not taken such great strides as now. The charm of Sawan, the rainy month, the music one gets to hear at the dargah qawwalis, the nuances of the erstwhile dancing girls, the *Sufiana* tradition, little known anecdotes about the Mughals, Diwali, Id, Janmashtami celebrations in times past, the glory days of Majestic cinema where, to see a show in the beginning of the last century, dhobis sold their bullocks and *bhistis* their *mashaqs* or waterskins, the exodus of poets, dancers and artists from Delhi to Awadh in the days of Nawab Wajid Ali Shah, and much more is in store for the curious.

Often called the 'Omar Khayyam of the concrete jungle of Delhi', Smith, a hereditary journalist whose father, brothers and sisters were also into journalism, never ceases to disappoint. I, as an old Delhiwallah with long-time links with the city, have great pleasure in recommending his book to all those who care for a good read. They will get to know so much about the quaint secrets of the galis, *kuchas* and monuments of Delhi.

O.P. Jain
Intach Convener
New Delhi

INTRODUCTION

Delhi has been described as the 'beloved of many and mistress of none'. I would beg to differ—'mistress' has an illicit connotation; the word 'wife', I think, would have been a better substitute. I shall leave it to you to ponder over.

The city was not really 'Alam mein intikhab' in the early 1960s, but the old order was, by and large, still partly in tact, and I'm a witness to its breaking up as also the big change when Delhi College was moved to its present location and renamed after Dr Zakir Husain. Wonder if Mirza Ghalib was alive if he would have got appointed as a teacher!

Delhi's old-world charm lingers, despite the many changes modernisation has brought about. But it was not so for me when I came to the city, to permanently settle down in it, in 1962, for I could not shake off my love for Agra. So much so that I went to it every weekend and came back rejuvenated after meeting family and friends, soaking in the ambience of the Taj and its environs. Even the *kharbuzas* (musk melon) of Delhi did not taste as sweet as the ones back home, and the *nahari*, *seekh kababs* and biryani of Nai ki Mandi and Naye Basti were far superior to the one available near the Civil Lines, where I stayed with my brother and sister-in-law, both teachers at St. Xavier's.

To tell you the truth, I felt very lonely as a bachelor during that time. It was difficult to pass the morning hours after a night shift at the PTI office in Parliament Street, when not courting an English girl teaching in a Mandir Marg school. So to while away the time, I got hold of my father's old bicycle, which had been languishing in the brother's verandah after he dumped it there.

My father, Thomas Smith, had been in journalism since 1928—a profession my brothers and sisters pursued as well before they took to teaching. The bicycle was originally a present from American journalist, Dorothy, Wittenberger, who had come all the way to Agra on it from Bombay about 80 years ago—just shows how much safer roads were then. A 'Hopper' model, it served the purpose of taking me around, surveying old monuments, starting with the Red Fort.

When I had to leave the staff quarters, I took the steel trunk (my only possession), caught an auto-rickshaw and landed up at Naaz Hotel, behind the Jama Masjid, where I took a room right at the top. This was the time when Pandit Nehru died. The waiters informed me that it had been occupied by the painter M.F. Husain before he became famous. I liked the room as it gave a bird's-eye view of the whole area, but the charges were so high that I was forced to move to the modest Azad Hind Hotel near Jagat Cinema, soon.

This hotel belonged to Afzal Peshawari who had seven wives and 28 children. Whenever the wives started fighting among themselves, I used to take shelter in Edward Park and then walked down to the steps of the Jama Masjid to eat *kababs* and drink water from the *jhun-jhun katora-wala bhistis*. By the time I returned the commotion used to die down and Afzal Sahib would be busy reciting poetry to women who came to buy chandeliers from the shop attached to the hotel, under the charge of his Christian wife, 'Memsahib'.

For years I stayed in this hotel—even after I got married. One of my sons was born there while I was on a visit to Agra. A midwife from Macchliwalan helped in the delivery at midnight, thanks to the sympathetic hotel manager, Riyasat—God bless him—and his wife, the ubitiquitous Mumani, a heartthrob.

Josh Malihabadi, the renowned Urdu poet, incidentally, was my neighbour at the hotel for three months. After dinner, procured from Moti Mahal restaurant, which he washed down with three pegs of Scotch, Josh retired for the night at 8 pm, to get up at 4 am to write his *kalaam* while sipping tea. He shared the room with his brother, the Khan Sahib who had continued to stay at Malihabad even after 1947. Josh's wife, who had come with him from Lahore, occupied an adjacent room, keeping a strict watch on him.

Poets like Maikash Akbarabadi, Betab, Madhosh and Gulzar Dehlvi came to meet him as he sat on a chair in the courtyard, sharing the hookah with Khan Sahib. That was the year 1967, if I'm not mistaken. Ustad Latafat Hussain Khan, who occupied a room downstairs, sometime sang in his magestic voice. Feroz Kanchwala, the singer with a glass eye; Naseem Bano, who had entertained President Najibullah at a soiree in Kabul; danseuse Shanta Rani, and visiting dance and music troupes from Bombay and Calcutta also made me prolong my stay at the hotel. However, my bachelor-day friends were convinced that I had fallen in love with the proprietor's pretty daughter.

Soon, I started loving Delhi and rediscovering its charms with my children who had to eat *pulao-zarda* brought from a shop everyday (as no cooking was allowed in the hotel) for lunch, while dinner was at Karim's. When they went to visit relatives they would naturally ask for *dal-bhat* or *chutney-roti*.

My connection with Agra started showing signs of breaking up as my parents died—my brothers and sisters got married and went their way, and friends scattered, some going away to Pakistan and others to the US, Canada and Britain or to Bombay, Calcutta and Madras.

Slowly, I became a full-fledged Delhiwallah, thanks to evenings spent at Haji Hotel, opposite the Jama Masjid. There Haji, Zahooruddin, who had been goalkeeper of Young Men's Football club, used to hold court. He was a keen *shikari* and had hunted right up to the Terai jungles. The deer he shot provided venison from which *shammi kababs* were made, not only for family and friends, but also for dignitaries like the Nizam, the Nawab of Rampur, the Viceroy and the Deputy Commissioner of Delhi.

Present at the evening meetings were Mohammad Mian Akbar, a shoe merchant of note, Bhai Alimo, Ustad Zahooro, Master Sahib and Mian Alamgir who had the facial features of Emperor Aurangzeb. The discussions ranged from the days of the Mutiny to the Majestic Theatre in Chandni Chowk—where, it is told, to see a show dhobis sold their bullocks and *bhistis* their *mashaqs* or waterskins. They were fascinated by Sohrab Modi, Mehtab, Prithviraj Kapoor and Zohra Bai Ambalewali. Discussions over, everybody dipped their hands into the big tiffin carrier, which contained Hajiji's dinner, and then departed still arguing on the road, while I made my way to Karim paanwallah's shop.

While passing through Urdu Bazaar I used to see Mir Mushtaq Ahmed standing in the balcony after his sundowner. CPI leader M.O. Farooqui lived close by, and not far from him, Mustehasan Farooqi, caretaker of the shrine of Hazrat Kalimullah. At this mazar many evenings were spent by my small family and me, listening to the qawwalis being sung by the brothers, Chunnu, Munnu and Ibrahim. A regular visitor was barrister Nooruddin Ahmed, sometimes accompanied by his beautiful daughter Amina, who acted as interpreter to Krushchev and Bulganin in 1955. Chaudhuri Abdul Sattar, Municipal Councillor and Imdad Sabri were also seen there occasionally.

People thought it was necessary to relish Karim's *paan* every evening. He had been a wrestler in his youth and even after quitting the *akhara* taught youngsters the *daon-paich* (grappling tricks) in the afternoon. He would then go home from where he emerged only in the evening after an oil bath, his *kurta* scented with the seasonal *attar*. Though balding he would nevertheless have a lot of chameli oil in his hair and *surma* in his eyes. Arrayed thus, he would sit at his shop and prepare huge *paans* with *katha-chuna* (lime and catechu). Soon his hands would be red as though dyed with henna.

As people waited to be served, they admired the shop, washed clean every afternoon. There were glass panels with palm trees painted on them, pictures of the Kaba and the calligraphic names of Allah and Mohammad. But the pride of place was taken by a framed verse in Urdu which proclaimed:

Paan kehata hai sookh kar mar jaoonga main
Aye lab yaar gar moo na lagaya tu ne
(The paan says, I'll dry up and perish,
If lips, my friend, you do not taste me)

The shop, alas, no longer exists; the likes of Pir Yasin Beg, Haji Zahooruddin, Afzal Peshawari and their betters are also no more. However, the fact that the capital continues to draw researchers working on the city's heritage, or on focussed topics like the caste system among Muslims, gives an idea of the charm still exercised by eternal Delhi.

Visiting forgotten monuments continues to be a passion with me, for in them one is reminded of what poet Shelley felt on seeing the ruined statue of Ozymandais of Egypt, King of Kings and master of half the then-known world. Like him our mighty rulers have also passed away, but in their mausoleums sometimes one can in an evanescent mood, imagine hearing *qabar ki awaaz* (the voice from the grave), so well expressed in an Urdu couplet, quoted from memory:

Raunde hain misle naksh-e-qadam
Khalqian mujhe
Aiye umre raftan chod gaye tu kahan mujhe.
(O, destiny, where have you left me to be trodden upon by succeeding generations)

Such, alas, is the fate of emperor, clown and commoner alike and history no doubt is witness to it.

Delhi has two faces—one which we see every day and the other that is hidden and has to be discovered by lifting the veil. The capital of many kingdoms and now the seat of the Indian Government is the beloved of countless people because of its many attributes.

Ever wondered about the history of Chandni Mahal or why a nondescript area is called Zakhira? Chandni Mahal was one of the three palaces of the sons of Bahadur Shah Zafar, which later came into the possession of the emperor's *samdhi*, Mirza Elahi Bux. When the roof of Ghalib's house fell during heavy rains, the poet is believed to have vainly wished he could occupy Chandni Mahal in comfort, with its owner, till his residence was repaired.

Zakhira is said to have been a royal granary in Mughal days. In the decadent period of the 18th century it had a *taksal* or mint operated by the Marathas—the name still sticks to the place.

Sarai Kale Khan, in all probability, was built by a nobleman of the latter Mughal period who lived on to see the aftermath of the 'Mutiny'. But the *sarai* is no longer in evidence.

The more famous Kale Khan was a nobleman of the Lodi period, after whom Kale Khan ka Gumbad is named. But Kala Mahal was Shahjahan's temporary residence in Kucha Chelan when he was building the Red Fort.

Many wonder why a bazaar is known as Bengali Market. During the British Raj a piece of land was given to Bengali Mal, a Rajasthani trader, on which the market was built. Hence the name, although people from Bengal also live there.

Panchkuian Road got its name from the five wells that existed in the area once. You may still find one or two of them in the building that houses a school for the blind, and inside the well-maintained shrine of Hazrat Syed Rasool Numah, who came to Delhi in 1691, some 16 years before Aurangzeb's death.

How many know that the War Museum in the Fort once served as the palace of Mirza Jehangir—Bahadur Shah Zafar's half-brother who was exiled to Allahabad by the British. Why is Zinda Pir a living belief? Where was Langre ki Chauki, whose counterpart exists in Agra? Did a lame man really have something to do with it or with a mosque named after him?

Why is Bhairon still held in awe and what is the actual story behind this tipplers' temple outside the Purana Quila? Who was Buddhe Mian, mentioned by Ghalib more than once in his letters? His house was blown up in 1857. Was Buddhe Mian a secret agent of the Mughals or the British?

Jawaharlal Nehru has observed that every stone of Delhi has a history. This is true about the old monuments that dot the landscape. But not only stones, even people, street corners and stretches of roads have a history, some of it fascinating.

Was there a *bhoot bangla* (haunted bunglow) in the passage leading from the Ring Road to Daryaganj? Some *dhobans* (washerwomen) reported sighting a wailing woman at night with many infants during the Emergency when birth control measures were enforced very strictly. How did the belief that this woman was Janani Mata (Goddess of Fertility and Birth) gain ground? Many of these spots, including the red-light area, in G.B. Road, lack a written history and much of what is known about them is through anecdotes and gossip.

In which *kotha* of Chawri Bazaar did Lal Kanwar entertain coustomers before she became the mistress of Jahandar Shah?

Has anybody been able to discover the *surang* (tunnel) that is said to lead from Shalimar Bagh to the Red Fort? You can hear a lot about such things while standing in front of shops or sitting in the galis of the Walled City, where the best paan was sold by Karim and Bundu.

Sultan Ghari is the tomb of Balban's eldest son in Mehrauli, but the villagers regard it as a mysterious building, where one does not venture after twilight. A four-pillared monument exists near Hauz Khas, built by Alauddin Khilji on the orders of the Prophet who appeared to him in a dream, as he did to Iltutmish earlier and directed the slave emperor to build the Hauz-i-Shamsi.

In Kashmere Gate, opposite St. James's Church, is a mosque that was built in memory of Shujat Khan, a commander of Aurangzeb, who was killed during the Persian campaign. This mosque was repaired by the builder of the church, Colonel James Skinner, half of whose family from his first wife was Muslim and lived in Meerut.

Kamra Bangash in Suiwalan in Daryaganj is now only a memory, but a huge gate, with fish carved on it, marked the entrance to the stronghold of the Bangash clan of Pathans, to which the sarod maestro Ustad Amjad Khan belongs.

Bulbuli Khana at Turkman Gate has ceased to exist, but the grave of Razia Sultan is still there, a poor memorial to the only queen who ruled from Delhi.

Chandni Chowk has many havelis, one of which belonged to Bhawani Shankar regarded as a turncoat by the Marathas and protected by the British, who resented him being called *namak haram* (one not worth the salt he had eaten). Another haveli was built by Lala Chunna Mal, banker of the last two Mughal Emperors. In Matia Mahal is a haveli where Ghalib recited his *ghazals*, seated in the courtyard. Eunuchs still attend the *qawwali* at Hare Bhare Sahib, but the Seelampur brothers, who sang at it are dead.

Dauji ka Mandir was once famous for its *kheer* and *khichri* and in Urdu Bazaar was a hotel where a poet with seven wives and twenty-eight children lived.

And so Delhi, the coy bride, continues to lead its twin existence—the known and the unknown—and only persistent efforts can make one familiar with both.

WITHER DELHI

Think in this batter'd caravanserai,
Whose doorways are alternate night and day
How sultan after sultan with his pomp
Abode his hour or two and went his way

Omar Khayyam

Delhi grows like a rabbit's warren, because of its haphazard growth. The air is polluted, so is the water, and there's chaos on the roads due to the heavy traffic.

What used to be the heart of Hindustan, with open spaces, palatial buildings and gardens to enchant the eye, has become a city of dust and filth that flows through the gutters on to the road and eventually ends up in the Yamuna, making it one big sewer. The few improvements here and there hold out hope that wisdom may dawn later, and some of Delhi's pride restored, before Connaught Place decays like Chandni Chowk, and the devastation spreads to the newer colonies and posh areas.

Many schemes have been launched to de-congest and beautify Delhi. Sometimes, one tends to agree with Mir Taqi Mir of how the city was devastated. Yes, Delhi was indeed the pride of the world and garden of culture, destroyed by the lightning that struck it in the form of Nadir Shah—and of course many other adverse events during the decline of the Mughal Empire. The advent of the British saw improvement, but then came Partition and its many horrors.

If one stands outside Delhi College of Engineering, housed in what was once a palace of Dara Shikoh, what does one see? Desolation! Even the structures of the last century are in a dilapidated state, what to talk about the time of Shahjahan! Yes, Skinner's Church is better preserved, but what about the other buildings around, including the mosque and the verandahs on the opposite side of the road, with rooms on top that are reminiscent of Kipling's Shimla?

Wander towards the Kashmere Gate and feel despondent at its state of 'preservation'—it is a place where people relieve themselves, after the closure of the historic gateway to DTC buses. The Bengali Club at the side evokes memories of the times of Nirad Chaudhuri. One met him sometimes walking from Maidens Hotel to Kashmere Gate stick in hand and dressed in a three-piece suit.

Kashmere Gate was fashionable centre at one time. It is going the way of all human creations. And as you climb the stairs of the Kauria Bridge and the extension and descend the other side, you see more desolation in the name of haphazard development. Even the grounds of the Hardinge Library have been encroached upon. There are cars, scooter, buses, taxis parked on the grounds, and behind them are the crumbling walls of the havelis of Chandni Chowk.

Proceeding to the Jama Masjid, the shops and the dhabas make you wonder how Shahjahan could have walked up to his grand mosque this way. The environs of the masjid, particularly the Urdu Bazaar, with shops competing cheek by jowl, and the stink from the fish and poultry market make you beat a hasty retreat via Netaji Park, which had its days of glory as Edward Park. You cross the busy road at the risk of life and limb and reach the rear of the Red Fort. The Jamuna flowed here at one time and boats were kept at its banks for the pleasure of the emperor and his harem. Now the river has retreated and is no longer fit for pleasure boating. But there's been one heartening development: the coming up of the Delhi Chalo Park and the facelift to the Fort.

What would the great Mir have said had he seen Delhi now? And Zauq? Would he have insisted on living in its galis?

Life Before Shahjehanabad

Old Delhi or the Walled City of Delhi, is believed to have been founded in 1639 by Mughal emperor, Shahjahan who named it Shahjehanabad. However, the presence of monuments from earlier Sultanate dynasties in this area raises a pertinent question: Was this area, now known as Old Delhi, not already inhabited in the pre-Mughal times, or why would its rulers build so many of their edifices there? They would not have done so in absolute wilderness where only leopards, a wide variety of antelopes, hyenas, jackals, porcupines, monkeys and langurs roamed!

During the reign of Iltutmish, successor of the first slave king, Qutub-ud-Din Aibak, Hazrat Shah Turkman Bayabani had already set up his *khanqah* or hospice where Shahjahan's Turkman Gate was to come up later in the 17th century. It was near this saint's shrine that Iltutmish's daughters Razia and Sazia were buried in Bulbuli Khana. Every Basant Panchami a big mela, amid kite-flying, was held at the shrine.

In the Tughlaq period, Firoz Shah Tughlaq's 14th century hunting lodge came up where Bhuli Bhatyari ka Mahal or Bu Ali Bhatti's palace existed, on the ridge near present Karol Bagh. Firoz Shah also built his *kotla* or fortress opposite the latter-day Khooni Darwaza (Lal Darwaza of Sher Shah).

Paharganj, one of the main bazaar's of Shahjahan's time was, it seems, already an inhabited locality during Tughlaq and Lodi period. The Tughlaq Baradari and a Lodi Mosque on Qutub Road proves that there were people living there, otherwise for whom were they built? Surely not for the denizens of the wilderness. Similarly, in the Jama Masjid area, Bhojla Pahari, part of which was cut down to build the grand mosque, was not the preserve of dacoits and gypsies only. Some claim there was a Vishnu temple nearabouts.

In Chandni Chowk the Apa Gangadhar Shivala might have come up during the time of the Marathas, but legend associates it with an already existing ancient shivala, a small one, which devotees visited. Not far from it was the Afghan Fort on whose ruins the Red Fort was built—like the Agra Fort, constructed on the ruins of a Pathan citadel called Badalgarh, originally a Rajput fort. Sher Shah's son built Salimgarh before Shahjahan was born. This was one of the places Jahangir, camped whenever he passed by Delhi on his way to Lahore and Kashmir.

The Jhandewalan Temple beyond Paharganj had mandirs predating the Sultanate era, and one of them was built by Prithviraj Chauhan's daughter, Bela, which exists in Jhandewalan Extension. Incidentally, Bela's husband was killed in a battle with Sultanate forces, near the site occupied by Pusa Institute. It was a daylong battle. When word of her spouse's death was brought to Bela, she and her maids committed sati on the Jhandewalan mound below which is the Panchkuian Road cremation ground. This would mean that the Chauhans, after the second Battle of Tarain, where Prithviraj lost to Mohammad Ghori, had retreated from Mehrauli to the ridge area that made way for Karol Bagh centuries later.

Interestingly enough, Firoz Shah Tughlaq's eldest son Fateh Khan was buried in a mausoleum around which Qutub Road came up. Known as Dargah Qadam Sharif, because of the stone bearing the footprint of the Prophet placed above Fateh Khan's grave, it used to have an annual urs even during Firoz's time.

Why did the sultan build it so far from the *kotla* and his other architectural creations in Mehrauli (where he himself is buried)? Probably because his domain spread that far and beyond to North Delhi, where his observatory was located. And naturally his subjects were living round about. Kali or Kalan Masjid near Turkman Gate was also built in his reign.

So, is it not true that Shahjahan built his new capital on an already existing habitation?

Forgotten Heritage

Sultan Ghari, built by Iltutmish in 1231, for his eldest son Nasiruddin Mahmud who died at Lakhnauti (Bengal) in 1229 is, what some says, 'the first example of a monumental Muslim tomb in India, except for some monuments in Kutch'. The tomb was repaired later by Firoz Shah Tughluq. Situated on Mehrauli-Palam road, it is a maze-like monument with the character of a *ghari* (crypt) and a hidden staircase. There are other tombs also of the Slave period in this cryptic edifice.

Among the lesser-known monuments Khirki Masjid, a double-storied mosque, built by Junan Shah, wazir of Firoz Shah Tughlaq in the 14th century, has three gateways with imposing minarets. The building gets its name from the *khirkis* or perforated windows which have corresponding cells in the first storey. The pillared courtyard has nine domes. One wonders why the *khirkis* were built and for what purpose? Was the mosque meant for the exclusive use of ladies in purdah? Its fort-like structure gives the impression that from the windows one could watch happenings outside, without being detected or getting shot by a traitor's arrow.

The Begampuri Masjid in Begumpur village on Aurobindo Marg is another structure of comparable proportions, also supposedly built by Junan Shah who is credited with having constructed several imposing mosques before Delhi's Jama Masjid came up. It is said to be patterned on an Iranian design planned by the Iranian architect, Zahir al-Din al-Jayush.

The Lodhi Gardens, later developed by Lady Willingdon, wife of the viceroy, contain the tombs of some Lodi sultans. The Sheesh Gumbad probably built by Sikandar Lodi, the greatest king of the dynasty, is not a headhunters' monument but known so because of its glased dome, which takes its name from the Persian word *sheesh* (glass). The *gumbad* contains a number of graves which have remained unidentified so far but not that of his son Ibrahim Lodi who rests in Panipat.

Dadi-Poti ka Maqbara (grandmother and grand-daughter's tombs) on Hauz Khas Road is a puzzling monument. Who are these two personages? Their graves seem to date back to Lodi times. During that period graves built on a platform were those of members of the nobility. The Dadi-Poti tombs are also referred to as those of *biwi* (wife) and *bandi* (maid). This further adds to the riddle of this monument.

Badli Sarai, on the Delhi-Karnal road in Badli village, marks the site of an inn built in Mughal times. Here a fierce battle was fought in 1857, between the rebel sepoys and the Gordon Highlanders, an infantry regiment of the British Army that existed for 113 years, from 1881 until 1994) who are commemorated by a monument. Now only the gate of the serai stands as a silent memorial.

Roshanara Bagh has the tomb of Roshanara Begum, younger daughter of Shahjahan, who died in 1671. She was very close to Aurangzeb. The tomb was planned by Roshanara herself in 1650, with a beautiful garden, ornamental fountains and canals. Now a Japanese-style garden adds to its attraction. The garden-tomb houses the Roshanara Club, set up after the Third Anglo-Afghan War by the British, which organised the first cricket tournaments in North India.

Zafar Mahal in Mehrauli has fallen on bad days. Built by Akbar Shah II, son of Shah Alam, it was completed by Bahadur Shah Zafar who also erected its magnificent gateway and named it after himself. The pattern of the *mahal* is akin to that of Chhatta Chowk in the Red Fort and its gateway bears a faint resemblance to the Buland Darwaza of Fatehpur Sikri, which Zafar saw as a young man. The city was founded in 1569 by the Mughal emperor, Akbar, and served as the capital of the Mughal Empire from 1571 to 1585.

Tale of Two Delhi Gates

Delhi Gate at the entrance of Daryaganj, one of the fourteen built by Shahjahan in his city wall, has a quainter history than the other thirteen, though Kashmere Gate, Mori Gate and Lahore Gate saw most of the fighting during the Great Revolt. But earlier Kashmere Gate was witness to a big flow of wounded soldiers after the Third Battle of Panipat in 1761.

Delhi Gate did not see much action until 1804 when Jaswant Rao Holkar attacked the capital. His siege was, however, broken by Colonel Ochterlony who defended the gate and the wall extending from it to the Turkman and Ajmere gates. After the Battle of Patparganj, a year earlier, Lord Lake is said to have entered the city through this gate to meet Shah Alam but some historians differ.

About 54 years later, the rebel sepoys from Meerut entered Delhi via the Rajghat Gate (now no more). However, the British force under Hodson, sent out to arrest Bahadur Shah Zafar who had taken shelter in Humayun's Tomb, went this way and brought back the bodies of two of the emperor's sons and a grandson through it after their cold-blooded murder at the Khooni Darwaza.

How much importance Shahjahan gave to his Delhi Gate can be gauged from the fact that besides naming one of the gates of the Red Fort also as Delhi Gate, he ordered this one to be more sublimely built.

Going by oral history, two criminals were killed and their bodies buried in the foundation (something also believed to have been done when the foundation of the Red Fort was laid, though the number of condemned criminals was four or five). This was not unusual in those times when such a tradition was followed, probably in continuation of the one in vogue in ancient Egypt, where cats were buried alive in the foundation as the pharaohs held the cat sacred.

The story that the Delhi Gate, like the Kashmere Gate, is haunted is widely believed. While a White Lady (sic) sat outside the latter in a ghostly vigil after 1857, the haunting at Delhi Gate started 30 years later after the murder of a woman sweeper killed by her lover—a British sentry who had fallen in love with her and got offended when he learnt of her impending marriage. The woman did the sweeping early morning when the soldier was about to end his night duty. Others, however, think it is the peepul tree growing outside the gate that is haunted by a *churail* who at times startles passers-by with her jingling anklets.

The Delhi Gate in Agra, which was built between 1714–1716, on the road to the capital, by Mohammad Farrukhsiyar, is modelled after the older one. Of the two gates the namesake in Agra seems to have a more colourful history, though few are aware of it

Farrukhsiyar, grandson of Bahadur Shah I and successor of his uncle Muizzuddin Jahandar Shah, erected the gate at the instance of his patrons, the Sayyid Brothers, Hussain Ali Khan and Abdullah Khan. It was with help from these two that he had defeated his uncle at Agra to usurp the throne and finally got Jahandar Shah imprisoned and murdered in the Red Fort.

To commemorate his accession, he thought of building a gate in the city in which he had realised his ambition of becoming emperor. This Delhi Gate also has a mosque adjoining it. However, that does not prevent it from being haunted—not by a female ghost but by a pir (holy man) whose spirit is supposed to have been seen coming to offer the last namaz at night, in the masjid. The story goes that the pir was held in high esteem by Farrukhsiyar for bringing about his success (through his blessing).

A strange parallel between the two is that while one Salim Pehlwan who had gone off his head stayed at the Agra Delhi Gate, blaming a city dancing girl for his plight, another character known as Salimuddin Masood spent his days at the Daryaganj Delhi Gate, lamenting his fate after being thrown out of a Chawri Bazaar kotha by the pimps who thought his presence there was affecting their business.

One difference being the main Delhi Gate was never illuminated like the one at Agra that had a thousands lights (diyas) burning at it on Farrukhsiyar's orders. When his eventual successor—after two puppets—Mohammad Shah was crowned at Fatehpur Sikri, the new emperor made it a point to visit the gate, 26 miles away, to offer fateha for his unlucky kinsman who had been tortured and assassinated after a brief rule of six years. Some say this was as per the prophecy of Banda Bahadur, the Sikh general, whom Farrukhsiyar had similarly tortured and killed after quelling his rebellion.

Tale the Grass Tells

It's not so much grass that grows on Jehanara Begum's grave these days as shrubs. Her wish to be buried in a *kutcha* (mud) grave was duly fulfilled, though a sarcophagus protects it from the elements, open as it is to the sky, but situated in an enclosed chamber with perforated marble screens, south of the dargah of Hazrat Nizamuddin Auliya. Still when one sees it, one is reminded of the Persian poet Sadi's poignant lines:

I saw some handful of the rose in bloom
With bands of grass suspended from a dome.
I said, 'What means this worthless grass.
That it should in the rose's fairy circle sat?'
Then wept the grass and said, 'Be still and know
The kind their old associates ne'er forgo

Mine is no beauty here or fragrance-true.
But in the garden of the Lord I grew.'

No wonder grass springs up like hope eternal even on old forgotten monuments where no roses may bloom. Grass is never a deserter. That was why Shahjahan's eldest daughter wanted it to grow on her grave. Legends say that she had a lover, a poet, whom she could not marry because he was not a prince. But what about her sister Roshanara who also died a spinster? Roshanara was considered hot-blooded and was supposed to have had many lovers. They did not get married for the simple reason that their husbands could become claimants to the throne. This was generally true of most Mughal princesses.

Forced spinsterhood found an outlet in poetry and both Jehanara and Roshnara gave vent to their feelings in verse. Persian was the language employed, for Urdu was considered the camp language and was yet to take over its predominant position. Persian similies and metaphors like the *jaam* (wine-cup), the *ṣhamaa* (lamp), the moth, the mythical mountain, Kohkaf or Caucasus, and the bulbul were hardly considered alien at a time when the ambience at the Mughal court was the same as that of Persia, Arabia or Turkey. As a matter of fact, even present day Urdu poetry waxes eloquent on them-and who does not enjoy this escape to a romantic past so far-removed from the mundane images of the modern age?

Jehanara's was indeed a life of devotion. After the untimely death of her mother, Begum Mumtaz, while giving birth to fourteenth child, it was Jehanara who looked after her siblings and father, even though he had other wives. Even Aurangzeb, despite the animosity she aroused in him because of her identification with the cause of Dara Shikoh, looked up to her as his *apa* (beloved elder sister). Roshanara was jealous but continued to maintain a love-hate relationship with her.

Even such a selfless person as Jehanara must have no doubt yearned for someone who could be the master of her heart. Her emotions are portrayed in her poetry which is that of a pious woman deeply attached to her maker. She was also a great lover of gardens and laid the Begum Bagh in Delhi in which was situated in the Begum Sarai. Outside the bagh was the Chandni Chowk which was also her creation. One can imagine the artistic sensibilities of the person who built this street where the moonlight was reflected in a central pool.

A French physican and traveller, François Bernier, records:

> If there is any street in the East where the splendours of the Arabian Nights are still credible, it is Chandni Chowk. For here are emeralds as big as turkey's eyes, palaces with golden roofs, female slaves who sing like nightingales, afrits and enchanting princesses.

After Aurangzeb came to power, Jehanara preferred to stay with her father, who was held captive in the Agra Fort for seven years until his death on 16 January 1666. She became a recluse after that and patronised mystics and mendicants until her own death. As per her wishes she was buried in the tomb she had built for herself in 1681, next to the shrine of the saint she held in such high regard.

The hollow sarcophagus is the receptacle in which the grass grows in accordance with her epitaph, which translated into English means: 'Let naught cover my grave save the green grass, for grass will suffice as a covering for the lowly.'

And yet she was the one who was once the virtual ruler of Hindustan and whose *paan-dan kharch* (betel leaf expenses, literally, but pin-money in this case) was met by the revenue of two flourishing ports of the Mughal Empire. Sleep well gentle princess.

Paharganj's Chequered Past

Paharganj's chequered past is not so well known. Before the railways divided the area, there was a direct road from it to the Red Fort on which such personalities as Sheikh Ibrahim Zauq (1789–1854) went by palanquin to meet the Mughal emperor, Bahadur Shah Zafar.

This Urdu poet and scholar, who wrote poetry under the *nom de plume* Zauq, had been appointed the poet laureate of the Mughal Court in Delhi at a young age and was given the title of 'Khaqani e Hind' (The Khaqani of India) by the last Mughal emperor, Bahadur Shah Zafar who was his disciple

Being the ustad who wetted the emperor's poety, Zauq, during his lifetime, enjoyed a status higher than that of even Ghalib whose unconventional poetry did not enjoy the patronage of the high and mighty and was left for the hoi polloi to hail the poet as a trendsetter.

Zauq's house in Paharganj can not be traced now nor his grave that was demolished by vandals in 1947 and a public latrine built over it for refugees from Punjab. But of late the place has been cleared of this monstrosity and a memorial erected to mark the last resting place of the badshah's ustad, though god knows where his bones are interred.

This is unfortunate as he was a great lover of Delhi who even rejected a lucrative offer from the Nizam to settle down in Hyderabad.

There were others of note living in Paharganj, like the descendants of Ghaziuddin Khan, the ancestor of the nizams of Hyderabad and the builder of the Ghaziuddin Madarsa at Ajmeri Gate—the first such institution of its kind in the 18th century. Ghaziuddin was the Commander-in-Chief at the Siege of Golkonda Fort in 1686 when Emperor Aurangzeb personally conquered Golkonda Sultanate

From the side of the gate the road led to Jhandewalan, past the bazaar which was the last habitation point on the Paharganj ridge before the rocky formation that marked its boundary was cut down and Karol Bagh came into being.

Paharganj, located just west of New Delhi Station, literally meaning hill-market, was once an important suburb of Shahjehanabad. It was one of five main bazaars of Delhi, and the only one outside the Walled City. Besides, it was the principal grain market in the 17th century and had the custom house of the emperor, for collecting taxes.

In the Mutiny papers it was referred to as Jaisinghpura or Shahganj. Muin-ud-Din Husain Khan, a cousin of Mirza Ghalib was the *thanedar* or the SHO of the Paharganj police station during that time and is supposed to have helped in saving Sir Theophilus Metcalfe's life during the uprising by sheltering him. It was in disguise that the hated Metcalfe escaped from the thana to eventually find refuge in Rajputana, which was not affected by the First War of Independence.

In 1920, when Lutyens was assigned to build New Delhi, Paharganj saw a facelift of sorts. Imperial Theatre, an archaic landmark, was built in 1930. When Imperial Cinema started showing films in 1933, the audience took its time to come in for the then-silent shows. Screenings did not start at fixed times, but had to wait for enough people to come in. Those waiting for the hall to fill up were entertained by dancing girls, performing in front of the screen. Early in its history, cinema drew the same moral censure as the tawaif's bordello.

Paharganj saw the bloodiest riots in 1947, a metamorphosis, when one community was forced to desert its roots and the other fled from Pakistan to make a new beginning here. Many took up the food business and soon became known for their products. Some of the famous names established since 1947–48 in the eatery business are still doing well even when the third generation has taken over. Pehalwan da Hotel and Sitaram Bhaturewala are among them.

During the hippie movement in the 70s, the area became a regular part of the hippie trail, with backpackers and college students looking for modest accommodation near Connaught Place. The legacy continues even today, with its budget hotels, cafes and restaurants, specialising in global cuisines, and a horde of cyber cafes. Of late, actors and actresses from the West like Kate Winslet of *The Titanic* fame have lodged in Paharganj during their sojourn in Delhi. The area has shelters and homes run by Salaam Balak Trust, an NGO for street and working children. Heritage walks are held to make the new generation aware of the area's past.

Ram Nagar at the eastern end of Paharganj was the first organised colony for officers of the Controller and Auditor General of India. It was outside the old city and came up in the 1930s. The area belonged to Ram Swaroop, an ice factory owner who was a friend of Ram Saran Das, as per the latter's son, V.K. Gupta, according to heritage activist Sureka Narain.

Ram Saran Das belonged to Bulandshahr and came to attend the 1911 Durbar. In 1913, he was transferred to Delhi as an officer in the Controller and Auditor General's office and initially lived in Sitaram Bazaar. He was also instrumental in building Birla Mandir and obtained special permission from Lord Willingdon, the Viceroy, to build Ram Nagar. The place was called Ram Nagar after Ram

Swaroop and Ram Saran Das. Building No. 11, Ram Nagar, was the first building built in 1934 by Ram Saran Das. These two may be regarded as the first colonisers of Delhi who lent a semblance of modernity to decaying Paharganj, whose bridge was once known as the place where missing persons could be found.

The Mughal Quadrangle

Delhi gave birth to the Mughal culture of Awadh, Hyderabad and Bengal. Though the latter emperors had little control over these important *subahs* (provinces) of the empire, their patronage was still sought by them. The nawabs of Awadh and Bengal began to flourish as did the nizams of Hyderabad Artists, musicians, poets, soldiers of fortune, dancing girls and eunuchs, besides artisans, merchants and clerics were glad to leave Delhi and make their new abode in the three distant principalities.

The greatest Urdu poet of that time, Mir Taqi Mir, who was born in Agra in 1723, lived much of his life in Kucha Chelan, Old Delhi. He moved to the court of Asaf-ud-Daulah in Lucknow in 1782, at the king's invitation. When his decadent Mughal nobleman's dress, manners and un-Awadh-like appearance became a matter of ridicule, at a mushaira he berated the *sakins* of *Purab* or the custodians of the East with the famous eulogy:

Dilli jo ek shahr tha
Alam mein intakhaab
Rahte the muntakhib jahan rozgaar ke
Jisko falak ne loot ke bezaar kar diya
Hum rahnewale hain usi ujre dayar ke.
(Delhi the premier city of the world, which was devastated by heaven's wrath and made into a desolate garden, I'm a resident of that ruined place)

His critics bowed to the great *shayar* (poet). However, the artists and dancing girls who had left for Lucknow found good pastures. One observer commented:

> The balconies of Chawri Bazaar lie deserted during the day and when the evening lamps are lit the *mujra* is heard only in some of them, while at the rest of the *kothas*, sans customers, the dancing girls keep beating their breasts and pining for new climes to the refrain of '*Hai nigori, Awadh jana hai*' (Oh, wretch have to go to Awadh), where *randis* became princesses overnight.

There were several instances when that actually happened. Khas Mahal for instance, one of Wajid Ali Shah's favourite wives, had an interesting background.

Khas Mahal, apparently the niece of Ali Naqi Khan the great-grandson of the Emperor, Shah Alam II, also had an Anglo-Indian grandmother, Sally—'the illegitimate daughter of an ex-British Resident of Lucknow, Gabriel Harper and an unknown Indian woman', writes Dr Rosie Llewellyn Jones in her latest treatise, *The Last King in India—Wajid Ali Shah*.

Sally, at the age of 13, had become the companion of Maj-Gen Claude Martin, one of the several 'adopted' girls in his harem. She got 'a generous life-time pension' from Martin before his death, in 1800, and landed up pregnant in Calcutta, where she gave birth to a daughter. It is quite apparent that dancing girls from Delhi had managed to establish contact with the Awadh's royals after moving there for a better life. Some ven went as far away as Mushirdabad in Bengal founded by Murshid Quli Khan, a Mughal governor.

Hyderabad had been created by a Mughal nobleman, Asaf Jah, whose father, Ghazi ud-Din Khan, lies buried near the madarsa he established at Ajmere Gate. He happens to be an ancestor of Delhi's present Lt-Gov, Najeeb Jung. Chawri Bazaar is not far from the gate and dancing girls from it went to Hyderabad too, to make the nights of the new state as redolent as those of the city of Mir and Ghalib and thus sustained the Golden Quadrangle of Delhi, Awadh, Bengal and Hyderabad.

As for Hyderabad, though many a poet and poet-taster hurried there, Ghalib stayed put in Ballimaran and so also Skeikh Ibrahim Zauq in Paharganj, the latter commenting,

In dinon garche Dakkan mai hai qadr-e-sukhan
Kaun jaye 'zauq' par Dilli ki galiyan chhod ke

> (Nowadays Deccan is good and prosperous, but who wants to leave the streets of Delhi?)

And yet had he lived longer and seen the havoc of the Mutiny of 1857, with both the rebels and the British laying waste Delhi, he may have changed his opinion of the imperial city.

Quaint Reminders of 1857

There are many relics of the events of 1857 in Delhi, both in the Walled City and outside it on the Ridge and the surrounding area. Whenever 11 May comes around one is reminded of them—for on that fateful day, Delhiwallahs temporarily shrugged off the British yoke and made the surviving firangis flee for their lives. And yet, at times, faithful Indian servants came to their aid.

In his book *The Great Mutiny of 1857,* Christopher Hibbert writes that when the British fugitives from Delhi were hurrying on their way to Karnal or some other nearby town,

> The four children of Captain William Wallace were spirited away by a faithful *khansaman* and found their way to Meerut. The merchant, James Morley, whose family had been killed in his house in the Kashmere Bazaar, put on a petticoat and veil, belonging to the wife of his old dhobi, and following the dhobi, as he drove a bullock laden with old clothes through one of the city gates, managed to reach Kurnaul road.

Another story goes about a lady who put on a *pugree* and dressed as a villager, with a small hookah in hand, and made her way out of town. She was recognised by her ex-cook who wanted to make the amply-built memsahib his second wife. But she gave him the slip at night and somehow reached Flagstaff Tower on the Ridge.

A girl, who had been disguised as a rustic boy, was kidnapped on her way to Sonepat by a group of eunuchs who planned to sell the youngster to a gay zaminder. When the man discovered that the 'boy' was actually a girl, he told his sister to take care of her until such time as he could secure ransom for her release.

All this happened 157 years ago but still comes to mind as one wanders over Delhi, to piece together quaint events, of which the nikah of a sepoy with the wife of a sahib he had killed is probably the most interesting one.

The cannonading marks on the walls of the Kashmere Gate and the fierce attack on Mori Gate, where the maulvi of Faizabad, Ahmedullah Shah, stayed, before the outbreak on his arrival from Agra, are vivid memories. It is said that the tall, gaunt, long-bearded maulvi, 'with coarse hair falling on his naked shoulders' and the same hypnotic gaze as that of the latter-day Mahdi of Sudan (or Muhammad Ahmad bin Abdallah, who led the rebellion against the British in 1885), however, did not stay here for long. He moved to the denser locality of Bara Hindu Rao and finally the Jama Masjid where, according to old-timers, he would be seen in the evenings; vehemently trying to convince *namazis* to throw off the British yoke.

Moving past Chandni Chowk one enters the lane of Ballimaran where the haveli of Hakim Ahsanullah Khan can still be seen with its old ambience preserved. The hakim was not only the personal doctor of Bahadur Shah Zafar but also his closest advisor, though often thwarted by Queen Zeenat Mahal, working at cross-purposes.

Some distance away at Lal Kuan is the Zeenat Mahal, ancestral home of the emperor's youngest wife, now turned into a school. At the mahal the queen had hatched conspiracies against the British. And not far from it Mubarak Masjid built by the *bibi* of General Ochterlony—an ex-dancing girl who later married a Mughal soldier, Wilayat Khan, and took active part in the First War of Independence.

Beyond Paharganj, in Karol Bagh, Rao Tula Ram School is a reminder of the brave ruler of Rewari, one of the key leaders of the Indian rebellion of 1857. His ancestor was Rao Tej Singh who sided with Scindia at the Battle of Patparganj in 1803, which they unfortunately lost to the British. After Tula Ram's defeat at the Battle of Narnaul in November 1857, the gallant ruler joined Tantya Tope and in 1862 and escaped to Russia.

Another hero of the Revolt was Raja Nahar Singh of Ballabgarh who blocked the road to Delhi. This 'Barrier of Delhi', admitted Sir

John Lawrance to Gov-Gen Lord Canning, was very difficult to break unless 'we receive reinforcements from China or England'.

According to Purushottam Salvi's book, *A Long Drawn War of Freedom*, Nahar Singh tried to persuade Bahadur Shah to take refuge in Ballabgarh, but the emperor refused and was captured at Humayun's Tomb. However, Nahar Singh avenged the death of Zafar's sons and grandson at the hands of Lt Hodson, by killing a large number of firangi soldiers. Eventually, Nahar Singh was captured and hanged on his 35th birthday on 21 September 1858.

One prince who escaped the vengeful British was Feroz Shah, who had been away on Haj when the Revolt broke out. On his way to Delhi on 26 August 1857, the troops in Gwalior pleaded with him to lead them. The prince agreed and captured Dhar but was later defeated, and after joining Tope managed to escape to Nepal. His not-so-fortunate younger brother was Mirza Nasir-ul-Mulk who became a cripple and was reduced to begging. Besides the more famous events of 1857, these remain half-forgotten episodes of those tumultuous times when Independence was almost achieved by the rebel sepoys.

Remembering Zamzama-Maker

Two days after the birth anniversary of Shakespeare and Wordsworth was the death anniversary of Shah Nazar Khan, the man who cast the Zamzama, about which Rudyard Kipling wrote in his novel, *Kim*: 'Who hold Zam-Zammah, that "fire-breathing dragon", hold the Punjab, for the great green-bronze piece is always first of the conqueror's loot.'

Shah Nazar Khan, an Armenian Christian, cast many great guns for the latter Mughals, but the Zamzama he cast for Ahmad Shah Abdali was the most famous. Abdali was also known as Durrani because of a *dur* (pearl) bequeathed to his mother by a dervish, who predicted that like the precious stone the fame of the child would spread *durr,* far and wide).

Working first at Agra and then in Delhi, where he stayed in special quarters in the Red Fort, Shah Nazar had as his assistants the gunmakers of Mohammad Shah Rangila who could have defeated Nadir Shah had he followed his advice and marched out to meet the invader at least 100 miles from Delhi. What was worse was that in a drunken state he rebuffed Shah Nazar as a heretical Armenian. From that time, the ustad planned to teach him a lesson, but since Mohammad Shah died, he could not keep his word and decided to make the dandy emperor's heirs pay for the insult.

Leaving Delhi secretly by night, he rode to Panipat and thence in disguise to Lahore, where he sought an audience with Abdali. Glad to acquire his expertise, Abdali, the man who succeeded the Persian Nadir Shah as Afghan warlord and was ravaging Delhi for long, decided on installing Shah Alam as Mughal emperor, entering into a pact with Nawab Wazir Shuja-ud-Daulah of Oudh, for the purpose. His biggest opportunity came when the Third Battle of Panipat was fought in 1761 with the Maratha confederacy opposing him and the Nawab Wazir.

Shah Alam stayed out of the conflict as he was still at Allahabad, where he signed the famous Diwani of Bengal with the British. But the invading force proclaimed him as proxy emperor. It was at this battle that the Zamzama, cast by Shah Nazar for Abdali at Lahore, was used for the first time and, rightly enough, in keeping with its fame, wrought havoc in the opposing force of the Marathas, with the Jats of Suraj Mal deciding to stay away as their guerrilla tactics were not adopted. The Afghans pursued their opponents up to Delhi and as far away as Bharatpur, where Mahadaji Scindia nearly got killed by a gigantic Afghan. He fell into a ditch which gave him a lifelong limp. Taking him for dead his adversary rode away.

Long after the battle, Shah Nazar is said to have returned to Delhi, working for Shah Alam. Some say he stayed in Kucha Ustad Hamid though it is more plausible that the master gunsmith resided in Kishanganj, which had a sizable number of Armenian residents.

He died in 1784 and was buried in Agra. Why he was buried in Agra is explained by the story that he wished to rest in the Martyrs' Cemetery along with other notable Armenians—among them Abdul Hai, Akbar's Minister for Justice, the emperor's adopted brother, Mirza Zulqarnain, and Khoajah Mortiniphus, a rich merchant and a great philanthropist.

Father, who traced his grave with difficulty had his epitaph, which was in Armenian and Persian, translated with the help of a Jesuit priest:

> This is the tomb of Ustad Shah Nazar Khan, the son of Allaverdy of Qaiquli, who was an expert in the casting of guns and who departed to the Lord with a good faith on the 25 of April in the year 1784.

The Persian inscription is on a white headstone while the tomb itself is of red sandstone. The ustad also cast a twin of the Zamzama, which was lost after falling into a river following a ferocious battle waged by Ahmed Shah Abdali. But the Zamzama could not be transported to Kabul by him and later fell into the hands of Maharaja Ranjit Singh, who used it at the siege of Multan and acquired the name of Bhangianwali Toph.

The 14.5 ft long gun, with a 9.5 inch bore is now parked in front of Lahore Museum, where Benazir Bhutto went to see it out of curiosity. Its possessors hold part of the Punjab, while the other half is an Indian state without the gun, to give a partial lie to Kipling's contention that 'who hold the Zamzama hold, the Punjab.'

Zafar's Bahu

One spent an entire day looking for information on Nawab Shah Zamani Begum or some trace of the house of Bahadur Shah Zafar's youngest daughter-in-law. Just as pretty as Zinat Mahal, she was felicitated by Mirza Ghalib in the *sehra* (panegyric) he recited at her wedding to Mirza Jawan Bakht.

Zinat Mahal's house still stands as a ruin in the Lal Kuan area. May be Zamani Begum too lived close by. But it dawned that the house was probably in Jaipur, her *maika* or maternal home.

Zafar and the Raj, by Amar Farooqui, seen in the light of the new moon peeping from the window, did contain some valuable information on the subject. But first about Bahadur Shah, fondly called *abban* in the zenana. Like his forebears, he too celebrated all festivals and enjoyed eating Twelfth-Night (after Christmas) plum cakes presented by Sir Thomas Metcalfe, say some records.

So much has been published on Zafar (1775-1862) that anything written now sounds trite, but Prof. Amar Farooqui's treatise, covering the period 1800-1850s, seems to be an exception. Talking about religious festivals, he says Zafar celebrated the two Ids, Dussehra, Diwali and Holi with great enthusium, being bathed in seven kinds of water and weighed in gold coins and grain, which were later given in charity. Only a buffalo and a goat were officially sacrificed in the fort on Id-ul-Zuha and the meat distributed to the poor.

For his own table, Zafar preferred venison from deer, shot by him on the Yamuna bank. A good shot, he trained many disciples to use the gun. It's a tragic irony that he could not even swallow a spoon of soup during his last illness. According to Farooqui, 'The abundance of game in the forest zone beyond Mehrauli, took the emperor annually for a prolonged stay to the Qutb, during winters. A routine followed since (his father) Akbar Shah's time.'

On 6 January 1851, Mahbub Ali Khan, Bahadur Shah's factotum, was ordered to prepare for the move to the Qutb. In Mehrauli he was invited by Mahbub Ali to look at a garden he had developed near the Minar. Bahadur Shah visited the garden along with his wives who spent the entire day there amusing themselves with plucking oranges—two thousand of which were sent to the Red Fort for the princes and princesses who had stayed behind.

Bahadur Shah then went hunting in the surrounding area, though he had prohibited the killing of peacocks and *nilgai* (blue bull). 'During the winter he would set up camp at Najafgarh jhil, accompanied by his wives, for a spot of bird-shooting'.

The one animal he had an aversion to was alligators, which abounded in the Yamuna and often preyed on humans. 'Fishermen had instructions to catch them so that they could be brought to the palace to be killed in his presence. A reward of ₹2 was given for every reptile killed'. ₹2 must have been equal to more than ₹2,000 at today's inflation rates.

The treatise gives such interesting facts and more, like how Mirza Jawan Bakht, Zafar's favourite son, died in Moulmein (Burma) of liver cirrhosis in 1884, as he had taken to drinking heavily. He had been sent from Rangoon to Moulmein to convalesce. His mother, Zinat Mahal, died in July 1886 of colic.

She had been addicted to opium for 17 years (probably to get over the tragedies she had suffered).

Jawan Bakht's wife, Shah Zamani Begum died in July 1899, when Jawaharlal Nehru was nearly 10 years old. Zamani Begum had accompanied the emperor, the queen and her husband to Rangoon. A year after Zafar's death, in 1863 she, along with her son and daughter, was allowed to visit her mother and other relatives in Jaipur and Delhi. She was to originally spend a year in north India but the visit was abruptly curtailed after three months as the British thought that her presence could lead to trouble for them.

She had arrived in December 1863 accompanied by a Mrs Cannon who then returned to Rangoon. The begum's mother came to Delhi from Jaipur to meet her. The Lt Governor of Punjab got to know of the visit in February 1864 and immediately objected to it, saying she should be directed to return to Burma, now that she had met her mother.

Later James Talboys Wheeler, Secretary to the Chief Commissioner of British Burma, who had taken charge of the royal family, suggested that Zamani Begum be allowed to travel to Calcutta with Jawan Bakht who could return after a month while she stayed back for treatment of a serious eye ailment that was threatening her vision.

Wheeler also asked for funds for the marriage of her 11-year old daughter. He had suggested a sum of ₹2,000 but the government sanctioned only ₹1,000. It also rejected the suggestion that Jawan Bakht should accompany his wife to Calcutta.

Their son, Mirza Jamshed Bakht (born about the same year as Tagore), went on to get an English education at the Diocesan school and Rangoon College and turned out to be a man of pleasing personality. He was associated with the initiative to build a mausoleum to his grandfather and was regarded as one who spoke the 'English language gracefully. He lived a life of genteel poverty,' dying at the age of 60 in 1921, some 22 years after his mother.

Had she had the good fortune of being the next Mughal empress after Zinat Mahal, Shah Zamani Begum's name would have enlivened history but *gayi yak ba yak jo hawa palat*, the wind suddenly changed. As for her ancestral house, it may be there in

Ghat Gate, Jaipur where some of the well-known Muslim families still reside, despite the noise pollution caused by the ironsmiths of Loharon ka Khura.

Dismal Times in Delhi

The affluence of Delhi, which was often the reason why others envied it or chose to ravage it, left it squirming in a despicable state, time and again. Before Shahjahan moved to Delhi, and again following the death of Aurangzeb, the the situation of Delhi was quite pitiable. Poet Mir Taqi Mir heard hungry princesses crying in the Red Fort, post Nadir Shah's 1739 invasion. The scene worsened after 1857, so much so that it prompted a foreign visitor to remark, 'Everybody in Delhi seems very poor'. Thanks to the British price agents (who fleeced the rich too) beggary flourished.

Delhi between Two Empires, by Narayani Gupta states that the local English newspaper urged the municipality to 'remove' the *chamar* and Jat women beggars. Such comments were not taboo then. Incidentally, Nazeer Akbarabadi's—the 18th century poet, famous as the 'Father of Nazm'—candid couplet was later to become the theme song of the Indian People's Theatre Association (IPTA) actors.

> *Sab thaath para reh javega,*
> *Jab laad chalega banjara*
> (All your splendor will lie useless,
> When the nomad packs-up and leaves)

Historian and author Dr Narayani Gupta remarks that 'removal of beggars would have involved removing the acute grain shortage and high prices' (so evident now too). However, one abjectly poor community, largely women, who did not display their distress, partly out of a sense of pride and partly, from a deep-rooted fear of the British, were the Mughals.

When the Society for the Propagation of the Gospel (SPG) missionaries began their work of educating girls in 1867, they made some headway with the Muslims of the Delhi Gate area and the Mughal princesses living in the 'nests of native hovels', near Mori Gate—an outcome of the fall of the Mughal dynasty. Hovels had come up in front of the Fort too, like the present-day slums around posh localities.

In 1861 the situation was so grim that 'eight thousand people queued for meals daily at the Idgah asylum'. In 1868, the Reverend Robert Winter of Fatehpuri Church wrote to a Miss Bullock: 'The servants are all crying out for an increase of wages'.

Because of the bad times thieving thrived. Though the Europeans in the Civil Lines employed chowkidars, not everybody could do so. Houses were robbed every night and the police were helpless. Begging even by those of good families was quite common. A separate entity were the fakirs at the Kotwali in Chandni Chowk.

A story goes, one woman who was slapped by an irate English lady, hit back saying, '*Khabardar, badshahzadi hoon*' (Beware, I'm a princess). Even in the 1940s those going out shopping were pestered by beggar women who ran after their tongas crying, 'Mai, give a paisa, my children are hungry'. Some would catch hold of a 'memsahib's feet' and not let go despite the tongawallah swinging his *chabuk* (whip). After the hurly-burly the beggars left satisfied, before sunset. I remember a bearded man, who looked like a retired munshi, and an old woman with an imitation necklace, pleading with those on their way to church (Baptist or St. Mary's), for a 'pleasing gift in the name of the God', every Sunday.

The most interesting story is that of a *nawabzada* who got the shock of his life when he saw his maternal uncle seeking alms with his eyes closed and an outstretched palm. He naturally walked up to enquire and was totally ignored. The next day the *mamujan* (uncle) came to admonish the nephew at his residence for disturbing him during his 'duty hours'. That was CID Inspector Sarfaraz Khan who was pretending to be a blindman while pursuing a murder case and in fact managed to nab the suspect.

The capital today has lots of impoverished people, some of them professional beggars, in a scenario reminiscent of bygone days.

The Medieval Inn of Arabs

Serais or inns have a certain fascination of their own. They were equated with caravanserais, like the 'battered one' mentioned by Omar Khayyam in his *Rubaiyat*.

> Think, in this batter'd Caravanserai
> Whose Portals are alternate Night and Day,
> How Sultan after Sultan with his Pomp
> Abode his destined Hour, and went his way.

Truly, many a Sultan made his way into it and went his way. The same can be said of Arab Serai, which has been renovated now by the ASI. Situated near the tomb of Isa Khan Niazi (1451–1525) an Afghan noble in the court of Sher Shah Suri.

This serai was built by Bega (Haji) Begum. Humayun's first wife. It is said that Humayun had left Bega Begum behind in anger when he took flight in 1540, after a tiff with her. She was looked after by Sher Shah, Humayun's rival and survived long afyer Humayun's return to Delhi with his second wife Hamida Banu. She was young enough to be his daughter but was persuaded to marry him so that she could give him an heir, which Bega Bagum had failed to do. Hamida did that at Amarkot with the birth of Akbar.

Bega Begum became Haji Begum after she made a pilgrimage to Mecca and performed the Haj. She was greatly loved by Akbar, Hamida Banu's son, and he helped her construct Humayun's Tomb and cared for her like his own mother, till her death in 1581.

One thing that is probably overlooked is that Arab Sarai came up before the completion of Humayun's Tomb. The 300 Arab workmen were housed there, just like the quarters of the men who built the Pyramids, which predated them. Similarly, the residences of the workmen who built the Taj came up before the monument itself. Historians think not all those who came with Haji Begum were Arabs, most of them were Persian artisans and also clerics, brought to pray for the dead emperor.

Arab Serai was the first halt from Shahjehanabad for those travelling by horse carriages via the Akbar's Grand Trunk Road to Agra. It was visited by Kipling after he had been to the tomb of Jahanara in

Nizamuddin and, seeing the grass and mud grave, was reminded of what Christina Rossetti, the celebrated sister of Dante Gabriel Rossetti of the Pre-Raphaelite group of artists, had wished for herself.

> When I am dead, my dearest,
> Sing no sad songs for me;
> Plant thou no roses at my head,
> Nor shady cypress tree:
> Be the green grass above me
> With showers and dewdrops wet;
> And if thou wilt, remember,
> And if thou wilt, forget.

It is said that Bahadur Shah Zafar was advised to take refuge in this serai and not at Humayun's Tomb as it was a better hiding place where the British spies (led by a munshi and a maulvi) would not have come looking for him, along with the notorious Hodson.

Author Percival Spear erred when he wrote that Hamida Bano built the serai and Humayun's Tomb, though she lived long and died two years before Akbar in 1603. Interestingly enough, at Arab Serai, which once housed an Industrial Training Institute, was the favourite stopping place for British couples who were not able to stay in hotels and were denied access to the Dak Bungalows. Captain John Foster and his wife were among them.

One story about Arab Serai is that it had become home for an Anglo-Indian artist, Eugene Dunn, who had come after his initial years in a boarding school orphanage. Dunn spent most of his time in sketching the monuments of Delhi, starting with Humayun's Tomb and working his way to Shahjehanabad, where he fell in love with the Moti Masjid of the Red Fort, describing it as a begum sitting in repose. But somehow he did not frequent Mehrauli as the Nizamuddin area with its serai appealed to him more. It was at the serai that he met his English girlfriend and went away with her to London during World War II.

There must have been others like him—artists, lovers and vagabonds who sought refuge in this 16th century caravanserai that had fallen on bad days, with only its imposing gateway beckoning tourists.

Historian Rosie Jones and the descendants of the British, killed or wounded in 1857, were among those who made a memorable trip to it 150 years later. Surely Khayyam's words still apply to the serai, though instead of sultans, common men and women stayed in it and went their way.

Its restoration will certainly preserve such memories and that of the pious Haji Begum who instead of bearing an heir, gave a beautiful mausoleum as a lasting gift to her beloved husband, with the serai as an added attraction.

Old Fort, New Mysteries

The Purana Quila is more mysterious than the Red Fort for the simple reason that it is not only older but built upon an ancient site, presumed to be of the Mahabharta times. So whenever excavations take place, interesting finds are sure to surface. Recently in 2014, relics of the 1st century AD, of the Kushan period, the Gupta era and the Rajput times have been unearthed. A 12th century Vishnu sculpture and a seal of Gupta times are among the prized finds by the ASI.

Besides the Vishnu sculpture, pottery of the Kushan and Gupta periods, undeciphered copper coins, terracotta figurines, micro-beads of semi-precious stones and glass, ear-studs and charred wheat and rice grains' have also been found. According to Vasant K. Swarankar, Superintendent Archaeologist of Delhi, the pottery products unearthed include knife-edged rimmed bowls, sprinklers and fragments of stamped pottery from the Gupta period. Also discovered are structures of the Kushan and Rajput periods. It all goes to show that the Kushans, imperial Guptas and Rajputs also occupied the site at different times.

This is the third excavation in the Old Fort after the ones in the 1950s and 1970s. The area being explored is the southeastern side of the Sher Mandal of Sher Shah. The Afghan ruler was not intolerant towards Hindus and did not interfere much with their religious practices. Neither was Emperor Akbar who later inherited the Old Fort.

Akbar's attraction to that town, associated with both Babar and Humayun, was natural, and the story of Akbar having got some idols transported from the fort to the Bhairon temple close by is not improbable. Though Akbar's Hindu wives influenced his thinking he had to be cautious because of the powerful ulema lobby in the court. He however, did not try to probe the mysteries of the Purana Quila as it was to Sikandar Lodi's Agra that he turned to build his own.

The Talaqi Darwaza in the Purana Quila was regarded as a forbidden gate through which everybody could not pass. Incidentally, to pass through the nearby Sher Shah Gate is like passing through the portals of time. In front is the Purana Quila and beside it the Zoo.

Also known as the Lal Darwaza, it is one of the many gates built by Sher Shah during his short reign. Like Shahjahan, he also adorned Delhi with impressive buildings.

Beside the Sher Shah gate stands the Khairul Manazil Masjid with a prayer hall, dome and double-storied corridors. The masjid was constructed by Maham Anga, Akbar's wet-nurse with the help of her son Adam Khan and kinsman Shahabuddin Khan. So the Purana Quila, the Sher Shah gate and the masjid make up a spectrum of history that echoes with the past. The excavations merge their own echo with it. If the site of the 3000-year-old Troy can be traced, why not that of Indrapastha? But for this excavations (now to a depth of 1.5 metres) it will probably have to be deeper than 12 metres to solve a long suspended mystery.

Red Fort Alcoves

The Mughals built their edifices with such finesse that even in this modern age of wonderful buildings one cannot help but marvel at their ingenuity. Take any palace in the Red Fort and one has to admit that its execution could not have been bettered.

The British tried to disfigure some of them and demolish others after the revolt of 1857. Following Independence, the Indian Army set up abode in the Fort. Its troops started living in the Victorian-type barracks constructed during the Raj era. Still falling short of accommodation, soldiers and their families were allotted the 32 cusp-arched alcoves or cubicles on either side of the Chhatta Chowk or Mina Bazaar. Now with the army evacuation, 22 of these have been reopened after breaking the cemented walls that had been built during the past 60 years or so to provide privacy to the soldiers' families.

One, however, remembers that not all of the alcoves had been walled up. There were some in which wives of army officers could be seen looking down at the visitors to the chowk. Among them was an old lady who spent most of her time sitting on an easy chair, gazing vacantly as though trying to reminisce of times when she was young and life was full of gaiety for her. There was a young one too who would keep eagerly looking out for her children, waiting for them to return from school.

Occasionally, celebrations were also held in these modifid homes—a birthday, an engagement or a wedding, or some other family gathering. But there were no loudspeakers blaring out and no disturbance was caused to the tourists who flocked to buy objets d'art, antiques, mementoes, trinkets and other souvenirs at the chowk.

During the Coronation Durbar of 1911, there was one shop which had a whole stock of photographs of those times, including one of King George V riding out at the head of a procession on a horse, instead of an elephant. Another much valued photograph was that of the king and his consort, Queen Mary, giving darshan to the people of Delhi from a balcony, specially constructed by Akbar Shah Sani, outside the Mussaman Burj near the Khwab Gah or dream house of the Mughal emperors.

The Khwab Gah is where the monarch took an afternoon siesta. It was Shahjahan's idea of relaxation after an exhausting morning and forenoon during which the two durbars, one in the Diwani-e-Am and the other in the Diwani-e-Khas, were held—the former was for the general public and the latter for the nobles. The emperor sat on the fabulous Peacock Throne during these durbars till 1739 when the invader Nadir Shah took it away, along with the prized Kohinoor diamond and other treasures in the fort. That was during the reign of Mohammad Shah Rangila, who used to sleep in the Khwab Gah with some newly-acquired concubine or the other.

The Chhatta Chowk, where the Mina Bazaar was held in the top and bottom shops on Thursdays, was meant only for the princesses and other inmates of the royal harem. No males were allowed, except for the emperor, though an amorous prince may have discreetly concealed himself from prying eyes to catch a glimpse of someone in the harem who had stolen his heart.

The arched alcoves above the chowk (built on the same pattern as the ones in the Agra Fort) were also used to display merchandise and jewellery. But some believe that they were meant for transacting royal business. One did not expect Shahjahan, with spectacles perched on his nose there, but lesser personages, the munshis and contractors, busy working on royal accounts and keeping track of the money spent on various things, like the daily expenses on meals, entertainment, grocers' bills, purchases from jewellers, money taken on credit (during the sunset years of the Mughal Empire) from the Seths of Chandni Chowk and the like.

However, some historiographers are of the view that the alcoves or top portion shops were also utilised for holding dances by the *kaneezes* (maids of honour) during the Mina Bazaar. Gossip would have us believe that the sound of *ghungroos* (ankle-bells), the beat of the drum and the silken voices of the singers could be heard right up to the *mardana* or male quarters, and no doubt excited the young royals.

When Jahandar Shah, grandson of Aurangzeb, ascended the throne for a year or so, before being assassinated by his eventual successor Farrukhsiyar, he had deputed Niamat Khan Kalan to play the sarangi in one of the alcoves. The sister of the artist, Lal Kanwar, had stolen the emperor's heart. He married her and gave her the exalted title of Begum Imtiaz Mahal, though she was a commoner and had friends among women who sold melons and mangoes or bangles.

No wonder then that in some of the alcoves bangles were sold for the princesses and their maids who, after getting tired of the bejewelled ones, yearned for common glass bangles, whose jingle attracted many a romantic heart among the princelings of the *salatin* or poor relations' quarters in the fort.

Now that the alcoves have been reopend, it would not be a bad idea if they were utilised for artistic purposes and not just left vacant for bats and owls to keep company at night. The sound of music, dances, skits and mushairas could add the much needed colour to the once vibrant Chhatta Chowk.

'Haunted' Havelis

Havelis, few are aware, were the mansions of earlier days and several of them still survive in Delhi, both in the city and in its outskirts.

Do you know there is an old building known as Haveli Sadr Sadur, where Ghalib often used to sit and recite in the evenings? Visit the place in the Matia Mahal locality of Jama Masjid. Seeing it you can hardly imagine that the building was once the haunt of the leading poets of the 19th century.

Built by Sadr Sadur, a minister of the last Mughal emperor, Bahadur Shah Zafar, the building has been partly renovated, though the interior is still dilapidated and is the home of several families who have been living there for generations, says Haji Mian, scion of an old Delhi family with a fund of knowledge of the Walled City.

Haveli Sadr Sadur was a very modern structure when it was built—spacious and well ventilated with side terraces and open courtyards. From the zenana where the women dwelt in Mughal splendour, one could watch the goings-on in the *mardana* or male quarters through partly-hidden screens and windows.

That period in history marked the twilight of the Mughals, but surprisingly enough art and literature flourished with a galaxy of poets like Ghalib, Zauq, Momin, Tischna, and Bahadur Shah himself, both exponent and patron of the Muse, says Dr Ausaf Ali, doyen of Hamdard University and well versed in the history of Delhi.

Except for the emperor, the poets usually came to Haveli Sadr Sadur as guests of the influential minister. And there were mushairas galore with the begums of the harem watching from behind the purdah the nuances of the evening, when the *shamaa* (lamp) passed from poet to poet and drew forth verse both jocund and pensive, or too philosophical for many to understand, and many just shook their heads, like folks do when puzzled.

We can imagine Ghalib at these sittings, holding sway as the evening advanced and the chandeliers at the haveli had been lit. But all this is past now and even bygone tales cannot impart to the building the majesty of thought and expression of those evenings. An old pedestal, where the lamp lit the courtyard, stands as a solitary reminder of the grandeur it had witnessed. The haveli, like all things which have had their day, broods over the many memories that haunt its precincts.

I stood outside it for some time thinking of the 1960s when I used to go to a *nahari* shop housed in it, run by a relative of the famous Karim restaurant. He used to wear a shabby jerkin in winter and dish out the curry, which cost just a few rupees, along with the rotis made on the tandoor, to his customers who liked the sizzling stuff. The man died years ago and the shop, Mughal-e-Azam, was closed. But even now one misses it and its owner who had an old-world charm about him.

Chandni Chowk has many such old buildings, some with gates that have outlived their utility. Take Katra Neel, which houses merchants and their shops, whose wares are much sought after by both the Delhiwallah and outsider, among them foreign tourists. The same is true of Kinari Bazaar despite its narrow street. But Haveli Haider Quli has its own distinctive mark and its history is worth retelling as it has been a residence without a break for some 300 years, which saw many ups and downs in its fortunes

At the fag-end of Chandni Chowk, Haveli Haider Quli is now a ramshackle building with a huge gate that yawns in the face of history. But there was a time when its owner was the big gun at the court of Mohammad Shah, lliterally so because Haider Quli was in charge of the Mughal artillery.

It is said that Haider Quli was a coolie who was made a courtier after he saved the life of the emperor's son. But this does not seem to be true. Quli is appended to many Muslim names in history though they were never coolies. The word coolie is derived from 'Kuli', an aboriginal tribe of Gujarat and was later used to describe manual labourers and then railway porters.

How he got that post is interesting. According to an old treatise, Hussain Ali, a nobleman, was Haider Quli's patron and introduced him to the royal court where he was given command of *atish* (artillery). Having secured the prized post Haider Quli was egged on by ambition to indulge in intrigues—a regular feature of 18th century Delhi

Besides other idiosyncrasies, one learns, Haider Quli was fond of fakirs and so mendicants found favours in his haveli. Among those was a fakir from Thatta, in Sind, who meditated at the shrine of Sarmad Shaheed, at the foot of the steps of the Jama Masjid. Sarmad, an Armenian, had trading links with Thatta before he came over to Delhi and forsook the world. The fakir of Thatta eventually became a conspicuous visitor to the haveli of Haider Quli, even as hangers-on do now.

Having got a hint from those close to the emperor that Hussain Ali needed to be done away with, Haider Quli lost no time in hatching a plot. The fakir of Thatta was made to dress up like a woman milk-seller and sent daily to the Red Fort where he came in contact with the mother of Emperor Mohammad Shah. With her help the plot against Hussain Ali began to thicken and the emperor himself became involved in it. So much so that when Hussain Ali was present, the emperor would speak only in Turkish, a language the unfortunate nobleman did not understand.

Then one day, while Hussain Ali was going in a palanquin, a hired assassin, Haider Beg, accosted him on the pretext of presenting a petition. As soon as the palanquin stopped, the intruder's accomplice passed on a hookah to the unsuspecting man while Haider Beg plunged a knife into his chest. He then pulled his victim out and cut off his head. A relative of Hussain Ali, a boy in his teens, witnessed the murder and immediately fired a pistol at the assassin, killing him on the spot. But the other conspirators, who were close at hand, fell on the poor boy and cut him to pieces.

History says, Haider Quli was rewarded by the emperor for the murder but was not a happy man after that. His haveli passed into other hands following his sudden death and today is a reminder of one of the conspiracies that marked the reign of the frivolous Mohammad Shah.

The address, '513 Haveli Haider Quli' has a fortlike appearance, but is today hemmed in by a rabbit warren of shops. It consists of three storeys with a concealed staircase for purdah women. The present occupants, Narain Prasad and his elder sister have descended from Raja Partab Chander, the founder of Partabpur, now known as Sohna, in Haryana. His decendants were uprooted during Babar's invasion. Garhmal Shah was the raja at that time. After he was killed, one branch moved to the court of Jind, the second settled down as Mughal munshis near what is now Mori Gate and the third went to join the service of the nawab of Awadh in Lucknow. The haveli was acquired by the family in Delhi during the twilight of the Mughals and ever since it has stayed put there.

The most romantic mansions in Delhi is however, the Namak Haram ki Haveli. Now a dilapidated building it was built in the Kucha Ghasi Ram locality of Chandni Chowk by a nobleman, Bhawani Shankar. He was the son of Rai Brij Lal and helped Jaswant Rao Holkar in the many battles for supremacy fought by the young ruler in the 18th century. In one of these campaigns Bhawani Shankar lost the fingers of both hands while trying to save his patron from a bayonet charge, for which he was amply rewarded.

But after serving Holkar long and faithfully, Bhawani Shankar switched his loyalties to the British who, in course of time, rewarded him for his services with a jagir and money to build one of the finest mansions in the Mughal capital. Looking at the haveli you cannot imagine how extensive it was once. I just stood there and wondered.

The residents of Chandni Chowk did not take kindly to Bhawani Shankar's action in deserting Holkar and started calling him *namak haram* (one who was not worth the salt he had eaten of his former master). Whenever Bhawani Shankar, now past his prime and further incapacitated by his maimed hands, ventured out of his haveli he was jeered with shouts of *namak haram*. This made him a nervous wreck as the ragging resumed when he returned to the haveli. Naturally, the infuriated ex-chieftain complained to the British who ordered that anybody caught teasing him would be punished. But this did not deter his neighbours from teasing him all the more.

Bhawani Shankar is long dead but the residents still refer to the mansion as 'Namak Haram ki Haveli'. As one passes by it one can almost imagine the shouts of ridicule, as they must have come thick and fast from both sides of the canal that once flowed through Chandni Chowk. And Bhawani Shankar, red with anger and shaking his hands, which once wielded a sword but now could not even raise a stick in his defence.

Not far from his haveli, facing the Town Hall, is the *kutcheri* of Bhawani Shankar. It was there that he held court as an honorary magistrate and decided cases concerning land disputes, inheritance, harassment of women by their in-laws, and also incidents of elopement, burglary and armed robbery. One can picture him in the mind's eye giving orders to the litigants and to the munshis who recorded them in Urdu and Persian—the court languages before English was introduced.

Isn't it an irony that Bhawani Shankar was unable to pass orders against those who kept troubling him? But sometimes they too came to the *kutcheri* to get petty cases decided. If the decision was in their favour they naturally stopped teasing Bhawani Shankar, but in private they still referred to him as *namak haram* or the turncoat. Interestingly, the sobriquet survives, perhaps because of the stigma attached to him when even the names of his employers, Scindia and the British generals, have been all been forgotten.

There are other havelis in Jama Masjid, Ballimaran and Kashmere Gate belonging to nawabs and seths. Among them is the Sharif Manzil of the famous hakims and the one owned by the decendants of Hakim Ahsanullah Khan, Bahadur Shah Zafar's physician and counseller, denigrated as Ganga Ram Yahudi during the Mutiny of 1857. Then there are the havelis of Begum Sumroo, Lala Chunna Mal, Haksar haveli, where Kamla Kaul wed Jawaharlal Nehru, the Skinner Haveli and the Kanjhola Haveli, all repositories of history. In Nizamuddin are the havelis of Mirza Jahangir and Mirza Babar while Mehrauli has a number of ruined havelis, all waiting to be explored by those of you who have the time and inclination to do so.

Monuments Awaiting Protection

Ninety-five monuments in Delhi are awaiting protection, but the Archaeological Department is still in the process of notifying them, says a report. One discerns a casual approach to the matter which has been long pending and resulting in more encroachment and despoliation of the capital's heritage.

Take the tomb of Birji Khan in Venkateshwara Marg, R.K. Puram. It belongs to a nobleman of the Lodi period who must have occupied an important post during the reign of Sikandar Lodi and accompanied the Sultan to Agra when he was trying to set up a new capital there. An earthquake and pressing matters of state hindered the work and the ruler's plans remained incomplete. After defeating his son Ibrahim

Lodi, Babar moved into the city and Humayun too camped there but it was left to Akbar to fulfil Sikandar Lodi's dream of a capital 122 miles from Delhi in the pre-historic Agravan, as Agra is known in Mahabharata times. Close to it was Vrindavan, now part of Mathura.

The tomb of Birji Khan, according to Maulvi Zafar Hasan, an ASI officer who surveyed Delhi in the early 20th century, occupies 18 sq. metres and has arched panels with a dome 'springing from a 16-sided drum, crowned by a marble and red sandstone pinnacle'. Its state of preservation is not good. Birji Khan's name and fame may disappear altogether if the monument is not saved.

Mohammad Quli Khan's tomb is in the DDA Park, Mehrauli. Vandalism and despoliation, despite renovation in 1996, are a big threat to the mausoleum. Dating back to 1610, it was built during the reign of Jahangir as a memorial to Adam Khan's brother, son of Maham Anga who was Akbar's wet-nurse. Because of this Mohammad Quli Khan too was a foster brother of the emperor.

While Adam Khan's tomb is fairly well preserved, this one is not. Incidentally, it was this monument that was converted by Sir Thomas Metcalfe into his summer retreat, Dilkhusha, in the 19th century. The British Resident made extensive extensions to it on the north and a pavilion in the centre. The tomb stands on the original wall of Lal Kot of Prithviraj Chauhan. Metcalfe also added many terraces and a waterworks. According to the Indian National Trust for Art and Cultural Heritage (INTACH), non-profit NGO, traces of a fireplace have also been found in the building, which has calligraphy on its arches and yellow, green and blue tiles.

Darvesh Shah's mosque, also in DDA park, dates back to the Lodi period. It is a wall mosque on a raised platform 'with seven *mehrab* recesses, raised battlements and flanking minarets'. There are several graves in the main courtyard, presumably of Darvesh Shah and his descendants. But who Darvesh Shah was can only be conjectured—a holy man of the Lodi era who was highly venerated, as is evident from this memorial, which however has undergone some renovation, says historian Y.D. Sharma in his book, *Delhi and its Neighbourhood*.

Hijron ka Khanqah in Mehrauli, DDA Park has a monument to an unknown nobleman and a whole lot of graves in the courtyard of eunuchs who must have occupied important positions in the Sultanate period, probably serving as chamberlains in royal palaces.

Bade Lao ka Gumbad in Vasant Vihar, behind Vasant Lok Market, stands on a terrace 4.35 metres high, according to INTACH. It has arched recesses on the inside walls and 'on the west a battlemented wall mosque'. The interior of the dome is ornamented. The tomb has become a residence in authorised occupation and may suffer more damage, which may result in the loss of this Lodi relic. Why it is known as Bade Lao ka Gumbad has not been established but the word 'Bade' signifies greatness of the person it commemorates.

Gol Gumbad in Lodhi Park is a tomb of 8.6 sq. metres 'and on each of its sides is a recessed arch, with a central doorway. The dome springs from an octagonal neck'. But this too is a monument to an unknown personality. So also Phutta Gumbad.

The Baradari south of Bade Lao ka Gumbad, has also become a residence despite being a tomb. 'There are 12 arches within the courtyard while the tomb has a domed *chattri*'.

The tomb of Paik is yet another endangered monument on G.T. Road. Belonging to the Lodi period it has badly deteriorated during the past few years—not surprising since it was formerly a police post. The octagonal monument has arched recesses and 'decorations on the neck of the dome It has openings in four cardinal axis' and the floor has caved in. *Paik* means messenger but nobody knows who this messenger was. One thing is certain that he occupied that post in Lodi times and as such was a royal messenger to suffragan rulers to whom he delivered royal commands and messages accompanied on horseback by a retinue of solders.

Turkman Gate, which has now been given a hideous coat of paint, is also awaiting ASI protection. It is a reminder of Shah Turkman Bayabani, the saint of the wilderness, who lived here during the time of Iltutmish and Sultan Razia and her brethren. Shahjahan honoured the Sufi by naming one of his 14 city gates after him. Should it not be preserved?

The Hanuman Mandir

The renovation of the Hanuman Mandir on Baba Kharag Singh Marg, which is planned to be completed by September, is not first such exercise. Historical records cited by Maulvi Zafar Hassan say the first known renovation took place during the reign of Akbar, in the late 16th century, under the supervision of Raja Man Singh, the most influential general of the Mughal army.

The raja was the one who had brought the idol of the Devi (Kali) during his Bengal campaign from what is now Bangladesh. This idol was temporarily installed in Agra and then taken to Amber, the old capital of the Kuchwaha Rajputs where it was setup with great fanfare. The idol is still there, with its face turned away. The story goes that human sacrifice in the form of death convicts was offered to the Devi at Dussehra, but in the early 20th century that was replaced with buffalo sacrifice. The idol did not accept the change and turned its face away in disgust.

The second historical renovation of the Hanuman Mandir, when a steeple was addel to it, took place at the time when Sawai Jai Singh was building the Jantar Mantar during the reign of Mohammad Shah Rangila in the second decade of the 18th century. Before that the mandir was confined to a smaller complex, dating back to the days of the Mahabharata.

It is said that the Pandavas came to offer worship there from Hastinapur and Bhimsen was greatly devoted to it. According to a legend, the strongest man of his time had a chance meeting with Hanuman disguised as an old monkey, with his tail covering a whole forest pathway. When Bhim asked him to remove his tail so that he could pass, the old monkey said that he was too weak to do so and Bhim should take the trouble of lifting it up and putting it on one side. Bhim exerted all his strength but failed and it was then that the old monkey assumed the shape of Hanuman. Folding his hands Bhim asked that the son of the Wind God help the Pandavas in their war with the Kauravas. Hanuman said he could not interface as he belonged to another age (yug) and that he should fight his own battles. So Bhim asked for a boon and Bajrang Bali assured him of his blessings and eventual success.

Sawai Jai Singh enlarged the old temple following a dream in which Hanuman is said to have told him that he needed more space so that his abode was not dwarfed by the Jantar Mantar. Make what you like of these tales, but the proposed Hanuman Mandir Vatika will definitely add the much needed lustre to the existing temple.

The Hanuman statue at the Karol Bagh crossing has become a cherished landmark, more so since the Metro started passing by it. Earlier, there was an idol of Hanuman on Shankar Road in front of a small temple, but it lost its popularity after the bigger one came up. There is a big rush of devotees seeking the monkey god's blessing on Tuesdays, but otherwise too, there is never an idle moment at the mandir with people coming for worship on all days and in every hour.

However, it would have been better had the idol been a little away from Pusa Road. Its present location adds to the congestion on the road. Moreover, the Metro line is almost cheek by jowl with it. May be in later years it will become imperative to move the idol back-and that may pose problems as it will not be easy to shift the massive structure without risking its safety. Another point worth pondering is the size of the temple, which is too small in comparison with the idol and spoils the symmetry. But that as it may, the Hanuman idol is a worthy acquisition for the capital and one which look long years to complete. At midnight when no worshippers are around, the pujari sits alone near the sanctum sanctorum, eyes closed in meditation and only a whispered prayer passing through his lips.

If gossip be true, that is the time when an unseen hand rings the temple bell, just an eerie jingle, which startles the pujari out of his trance and lends credence to the belief that Hanuman never leaves his devotees alone. The ringing of the bell at midnight was hitherto associated with the red stone horse monument on the road that goes past Akbar's tomb at Sikandra in Agra. Now the legend has moved closer to Delhi itself. But only a few know about it, and fewer still believe in it. Nevertheless, Metro commuters do turn around and pay obeisance whenever the train moves past this amazing structure of Bajrang Bali.

Saving Delhi's Heritage

Delhi's glorious heritage is fast getting eroded because of rampant despoliation, encroachment, urbanisation and neglect. Nawab Dojana's haveli, known as Dojana House in Matia

Mahal Street is now a flatted building which is already showing signs of deterioration. Haveli Sadr Sadur, bang opposite it, has been so encroached upon and rebuilt in parts that it is hard to recognise it. The haveli of Nawab Buddan, said to be a great fashion trendsetter, could not be traced perhaps because of alterations. The old hamam in the same street, which had become a shop, is also not easily recognizable. The building behind Jama Masjid associated with Dara Shikoh has become a school.

The monuments of Mehrauli that are not among the official list (despite Maulvi Zafar Hasan's classification) are slowly disappearing as most of the care and attention is lavished by the Archaeological Department on the well-known edifices. The same is the case in Nizamuddin area. The gateway of the house of Mirza Jahangir, favourite son of Akbar Shah II and Queen Mumtaz Mahal II, in the Nizamuddin Dargah complex is showing signs of deterioration. His tomb and that of Mohammad Shah Rangila (which look almost identical) are also showing signs of wear and tear. Mirza Jahangir is the one whose return from exile in Allahabad in the early 19th century resulted in the institution of the annual Phoolwalon ki Sair. The Tughlaq period Langar Khana in the same complex is a picture of neglect, as is the eastern gateway of the Dargah.

The two dalans or verandahs of Atgah Khan's tomb complex, which were used as *khanqas* or hospices in Mughal times, look dilapidated. Atgah Khan was the husband of Ji Ji Angah, also a wet-nurse of Akbar, who was mudered by Adam Khan, son of the other wet nurse, Maham Anga, out of jealousy. Atgah's mausoleum has, however, been renovated under the restoration plan of the Aga Khan Trust.

Bari ka Gumbad, east of Atgah Khan's tomb, is deteriorating, so also a gateway north of the Chausath Khamba. The gateway of Inner Kot, west of Kali Masjid, is in a bad state. It leads to a small fortification which, according to INTACH, once had the houses of the *pirzadas* of the Nizamuddin Dargah.

Khan-i-Jahan Tighlinani's tomb in Nizamuddin village shows signs of serious deterioration. He was the wazir of Firoz Shah Tughlaq and father of Khan-i-Jahan Junan Shah, who succeeded him as wazir. It is supposed to be the first octagonal tomb built in Delhi. New buildings have come up close to the tomb so that it is hemmed in between them. Junan Shah built several mosques, some say nine, others seven, in Delhi, of which the Khirki Masjid is one. A mosque similar to it was constructed by him in Nizamuddin.

Bu Halima's tomb is more of a ruin though the gateway is well preserved. But the same cannot be said of the gateway of Arab ki Sarai. The tomb of Sayyid Yasin of the Lodi period nearby on Mathura Road is another picture of neglect. Afsarwala tomb and mosque of Akbar's reign, dating to 1566–67, also shows deterioration. Afsarwala seems to have been a royal court official. The Sundarwala Burj, *mahal* and well of Sundar Bagh nursery are in need of better upkeep.

Bara Bateshwarwala Mahal and Chhota Bateshwarwala Mahal are also deteriorating. Bara Bateshwarwala Mahal has the tomb of Muzzafar Husain Mirza, a grand nephew of Humayun, who died in 1603–1604, a year or two before Akbar. The Chhota Bateshwarwala Mahal contains the tomb of an unidentified nobleman of the early Mughal period. Chilla Nizamuddin, north of Humayun's Tomb, erected by Firoz Shah Tughlaq, now has Dumduma Sahib gurdwara as its neighbour, and is a picture of neglect. So also the grave platform, east of Bhartiyan, built of Lahori brick and containing many unidentified tombs.

Gol Gumbad on Lodi Road and Khan-e-Dauran Khan's mosque, west of the Nizamuddin Dargah complex, are rapidly deteriorating. The former is the tomb of Khan Bahadur Mansur Jung, who held the *mansabh* (command) of 7,000 (horse) during the reign, and was a favourite coutier of Farrukhsiyar in the early 18th century. He died in 1739 when Mohammad Shah was on the throne in the year Nadir Shah invaded Delhi.

The Gumti in Kotla Mubarakpur contains a pavilion of Lodi times and is in a seriously deteriorated state. A forgotton tomb, situated off Mathura Road in open land, east of the Nizamuddin flyover, also of the Lodi period is slowly crumbling as it does not find mention in historical records.

There are many such structures dotted all over Delhi that are suffering neglect on that account. Yet, they too are the repositories of the capital's chequered past and could be saved for posterity if the ASI shows more initiative. Kale Khan ka Gumbad, in which is situated the tomb of Mobarak Khan, father of Darya Khan Lohani, in South Extension-I belongs to the Lodi period and is believed to have been built in 1481 during the reign of Bahlul Lodi. As such it is a monument that needs greater care than bestowed on it and on the tomb of his son nearby. Such grand monuments, had they been in some other country, would have been preserved with great care but unfortunately, this is not the case in India—and what more its capital!

Vanished Heritage Roofs

The decision to renovate and restore monuments in the Mehrauli Archaeological Park was long overdue. Though late it is nevertheless welcome. Among the tombs to be renovated is that of Ghiasuddin Balban, which dates back to 1286. Just like the older tomb of Illtutmish, this one also does not have a roof. But since mausoleums of such important personages could not have been built roofless, it is fair to assume that the roofs collapsed during the course of centuries after weathering many a monsoon or invasion by hostile forces. It would be in the fitness of things, if the ASI takes up the challenge of restoring them as also that of Alauddin Khilji's. This will no doubt be a daunting task as no depiction of these tombs, complete with the roofs, is available but architectural trends in those days and guesswork may be of some help.

When one visited the tomb of Alauddin, one found that a mongoose had made its home there in a hole. That was over 10 years ago. A recent visit to Balban's tomb revealed that a whole mongoose family was active in it. Illtutmish's tomb had a chameleon, a big one, which changed colour frequently, with it's throat getting knotty as if it was about to shoot the poisonous *goli* which, as erroneously believed, the *girgit* uses to attack those who try to impede its path. One of the caretakers, however, disclosed that mongooses are pretty common in the area and hide in Illtutmish's tomb too. And this, he thought, was a welcome sign since it kept snakes away, for no snake however, venomous would like to meddle with a mangoose. Otherwise, snake-bite cases in and around dilapidated monuments are not uncommon during the rainy season.

One thing that ASI must keep in mind while renovating Balban's tomb is that the slave ruler spent a considerable part of his life at his estate in Hansi (now in Haryana). Surely the ruins at the place if renovated could throw fresh light on this stern and able administrator. His palace, Kushaki Lal in Nizamuddin is in a pitiable state and despite some repairs is still far from being labeled as 'restored'. Sikandar Lodi's tomb in Lodi Park is also to be renovated but what about the tomb of his son, Ibrahim Lodi in Panipat, which can hardly be called a mausoleum, as it is just a grave raised above a platform.

It was built courtesy Babar who, after the First Battle of Panipat, sent out his men to find out the fate of his rival. They discovered the body of Ibrahim among the slain, for he had died fighting gallantly and the Mughal invader could not but salute his bravery. Babar had the body buried in a mud grave which was later built upon by Ibrahim's mother (the Sultana Begum). She had been taken into protective custody by Babar, who later allotted a special place to her among the ladies of his harem. But bent on avenging her son's death she bribed a cook to mix the dreadful poison *kalakuta* in the Mughal emperor's food. Babar became violently ill but somehow survived. The effects of the poison, however, it is said, led to his early death. A debatable point but worth consideration.

Ibrahim Lodi's tomb should also get a roof and the buildings at Sikandra in Agra, where Sikandar Lodi wanted to establish a new capital, too need to be reclaimed. The tank he built is now known as Guru ka Tal and the tomb of Khwajasarai Itibari Khan, the royal eunuch who tortured Shahjahan in his last days in the Agra Fort, has become a gurdwara.

Sikandar Lodi was the greatest king of the short-lived dynasty and preserving his legacy so close to Delhi should not be difficult. But one thing that no renovation can probably restore is the missing grave of Balban. The grave of one of his sons and that of another relative can be traced in the mausoleum but not that of the Slave Sultan's. It is said that he was cursed by a dervish that after death there would be no trace of his remains as he had punished a holy man on the mere suspicion of witchcraft. But this is just a myth. May be a successor king, the elements or vandals were really responsible for the vanished grave. Still it takes away from the sanctity of the monuments.

Skinner's House Needs Preservation

Colonel James Skinner's house in Kashmere Gate is in need of urgent repairs (172 years after his death), especially when recentlty a part (actually an outhouse) collapsed, resulting in the death of a woman and her little daughter and injuries to some other tenants. Part of the Bengali Club close by also collapsed soon after, as a further sign that the historic buildings in the area are in a bad state after encroachment and illegal constructions.

George Heatherley, a relation of the Skinners, used to come every year from Perth to see the place where his family lived for long and spend Christmas and New Year in Delhi. His death about two years ago meant the snapping of an old link. Now Prof Sydney Reberio is the remaining chip off the old block. He lives in Sarita Vihar, far from Kashmere Gate, but still misses the ambience of the old haveli which once housed Hindu College and his uncle George.

Colonel Skinner's attachment to the Kashmere Gate house was great, as it gave him access to the Mughal court and to Akbar Shah Sani, the emperor, besides the *rais* (wealthy) of the capital among whom he held a high place because of his connection with the British after he left the Marthas, notably Scindia.

This residence was also dear to him because it was there that he generally met his dearest friend, the British Resident William Fraser. How he and Fraser enjoyed each other's company has now become part of a legend. They spent time in planning hunting expeditions, sharing battle experiences and sexcapades, watching dances by the nautch girls and of course drinking long and deep, sometimes from afternoon to late evening when Fraser had to return to his mansion on the Ridge and on the way to which one night he was shot by an assassin hired by the Firozepur nawab, Shamsuddin Khan. Fraser's death in 1835 was a big blow to Skinner who really could not get over it right up to his death on 4 December 1841. The grave he built for his friend in front of St. James's Church is still there as a reminder of their friendship.

Skinner's Church, as is well know, was built in perpetuation of a vow on the battlefield of Oniara, also in Haryana, in which Skinner nearly died. It is worth mentioning the incident in his own words:

> The Oonehara Rajah soon became aware of the badness of our troops and crossed the river on the 25th of January (1800)...Two of the enemy's battalions came up to attack me but I charged and drove them away.

Later Skinner found that of his 300 men, only 10 were now with him. Skinner goes on to say in his memoir, republished by his descendant Brig. Michael, in 1955:

> As I was going to follow (search for) them (the other 290 men), a horseman galloped up, matchlock in hand, and shot me through the groin. It was about three in the afternoon that I fell, and I did, not regain my senses till sunrise next morning...I crawled under a bush to shelter myself from the sun. Two more of my battalion crept near me—the one a *soobahdar*, that had his leg shot off below the knee, the other a *jemiadar* had a spear wound through his body. We were now dying of thirst, but not a soul was to be seen; and in this state we remained the whole day, praying for death. Night came on but neither death nor assistance. The moon was full and clear and about midnight it was very cold. So dreadful did this night appear that I swore if I survived to have nothing more to do with soldering...the wounded on all sides, including his brother, crying for water—the jackals tearing the dead and coming nearer and nearer to see if we were ready for them, we only kept them off by throwing stones and making noises. Thus passed this long and horrible night (*Hijr ki raat*). Next morning we spied a man and an old woman, who came to us with a basket and a pot of water and to every wounded man she gave a piece of *joaree* (jowar) bread and a drink from her water pot. But the *soobahdar* was a Rajpoot, he would receive neither bread nor water from her (as she was of a lower caste) so he preferred to die unpolluted.

This was woman whom the Colonel from then on regarded as his mother.This is a rare verbatim account, part of the Colonel's memories written in Persian, which to one's knowledge has never been published in any newspaper to-date, and shows the plight of the man when he vowed to build a church as a token of his gratitude. To do that he had to live close to the site he had chosen and hence the importance of the Kashmere Gate house to him. He would walk across from it to the under-construction church (opened in 1840) before returning for a cherished meeting with William Fraser. Should not this building, spread over more than 500 sq. yards be restored and preserved by the Archaeological Department as a heritage site?

The Crowning Glory

The crowning glory of Humayun's Tomb, the finial on top of the dome, was uprooted in the devastating storm in 2012. The lightning conductor attached to it was also destroyed. A new conductor was installed but the replacement of the finial was not so easy, says the ASI. According to a report, it consisted of a wooden beam and nine copper vessels with a brass finish. The finial's shaft, made of sal wood, had been lost. So ASI had to source seasoned wood.

Records say the 16th century finial, installed at the instance of Akbar, who advised his step-mother, Haji Begum on the construction of his father's tomb, was repaired by the British in 1912. Accoding to Delhi ASI chief Vasant Swarankar 'The Islamic inscription attached to the finial stated:

> *Khuda jo hai, wo barkat rakhe, kisi bhi aapda se bachye*
> (May God always keep it prosperous, protect it from any calamity)

This talisman, like the one said to have been given by an Olympian deity to the city of Troy, was supposed to grant safety to the monument. Incidentally, when the luck of Troy was stolen by the Greeks, the Trojans faced one calamity after another and were finally defeated in the 10-year war, following Paris of Troy's elopement with the already-married Helen.

The belief in sacred symbols was not limited to the Greeks and Trojans. The Egyptians, Romans, Jews, Christians and Muslims were also influenced by it. Even the finial atop the Taj contains an auspicious *kalma*. Some years ago the 10 finials over the miniature domes of the Delhi Gate of the Red Fort were found missing. At the time when they were made by the same artisans who had worked on the Taj, their worth was not much but in present times they are valued at $42,000 each, as they are encased in gold. The finials of the Agra Fort escaped damage during the freedom war of 1857 (as did the ones in the Red Fort), but both buildings suffered extensively during the Jat and Rohilla raids of the 18th century.

Coming back to the Humayun's Tomb, the lightning conductor on it was installed after one was fixed on top of the Qutub Minar, which had been struck by lightning during the British era, and also earlier, notably during the reign of Firoz Shah Tughlaq who had the minar extensively repaired.

Haji Begum, Humayun's first wife, was a pious woman who went all the way to Mecca to bring back Arab artisans and mullahs, after performing Haj, to build the mausoleum and also pray for the repose of the emperor's soul. The *kalas* of the finial was set up after extensive prayers to ward off the evil eye from a thing of beauty. Its absence may rankle those who believe in auspicious symbols and also rationalists who may find it hard to appreciate the symmetry of the dome minus the finial. The sooner it is re-installed the better.

Believe it or not, one superstitious resident of the Nizamuddin area thinks an owl or some other bird of ill-omen sat on the finial and polluted it by its droppings, which induced nature to destroy it via a lightning bolt. One may laugh that away though not those who believe in such things.

When Bahadur Shah Zafar was arrested at Humayun's Tomb in 1857, Major Hodson nearly got part of the monument destroyed to ferret out the rebel sepoys he thought were hiding there. May be the blessed inscription saved it, just like the *tawiz* or amulet tied to Sipahr Shikoh's biceps supposedly protected the younger son of Dara from being captured at the fateful Battle of Samugarh, 199 years earlier.

Preserving Raj Emblems

Dumping of emblems of the Raj, which actually began in the 1950s, seems to be back in operation and the main target is Victoria

Regina, who though an alien queen was nevertheless regarded as a benevolent benefactress of the post-1857 reconciliation.

Delhi had a number of statues of hers, besides the one at the Town Hall which made the area look like St. Mark's Square in Venice because of the teeming pigeons it attracted. That statue did not somehow find a place in Coronation Park but in the Delhi College of Art. Others are untraceable.

The bust at the erstwhile Victoria Zenana Hospital was looked upon by women both as a symbol of fertility (the queen had several children) and as a talisman of sorts for a safe delivery. The *hajjan buas* or matriarchs of Jama Masjid still swear by Malika Victoria as the doyenne of womanhood and so do the *matajis* of Chandni Chowk, Chawri Bazaar and Daryaganj. As a matter of fact, Agra and other towns of North India also seem to habour this belief. The reason probably is that she filled the vacuum after the era of native queens and *badshahzadis* (princesses) with whom housewives could easily empathise.

Vying with Delhi for Queen Victoria statues were Calcutta and Agra. The latter had three magnificent ones, one of which occupied pride of place in Macdonald Park, opposite the Taj Mahal, now named after Shahjahan. One remembers being present at the park when the statue was being taken down in 1957 as father's Press photographer. This statue and the other two were deposited in the Police Lines from where they were recently brought to the local Paliwal Park, the earlier Hewett Park.

While Hewett was a high-profile administrator, S.K.D. Paliwal lived near the park after resigning as Food Minister in Govind Ballabh Pant's UP Govt, following his second marriage to a Begum of a well-known Allahabad family. The resignation was compared to the abdication by Edward VIII after his marriage to the divorced Mrs Simpson of the US.

It was planned to set up the Victoria statues in a Paliwal Park museum of the Raj days but Bajrang Dal volunteers had other ideas. They dumped them behind the nearby John's Public Library. This library, as per the Dal's demand, should be renamed after Dr Ram Vilas Sharma, a Hindi litterateur, who left Agra to lead a retired life in Delhi's Vikaspuri until his death at a very old age. It is pertinent to point out that Dr Sharma, a Communist leader, was actually head of the department of English in B.R. College, Agra and taught English romantic poetry with great relish despite his Leftist views.

The library was built by the John family, of Greek origin, originally named Joanides. Their ancestor, Antonious Joanides took the simpler name of Anthony John when he started life in the city of the Taj as a diamond merchant in 1801 and some of his descendents are still there after 213 years of habitation. They were neither British nor colonialists but philanthropic mill-owners who employed hundred of people in Delhi, Agra and Lucknow and gifted the library to the Municipal Committee in 1925, soon after its construction.

It is worth noting that after Victoria was crowned Empress of India in 1858, romantic as she was, felt that she had merely become ruler in succession to Bahadur Shah Zafar to continue the tradition of the Mughals. Though her desire to visit the country did not materialise, she had Munshi Abdul Karim appointed as her Urdu teacher so that she could understand her new subjects better. The munshi became a much loved member of her household and his father too, a doctor in the Central Jail, was invited to visit England and made Khan Bahadur. Because of her popularity is it any surprise then that countless girls in the country were named Victoria, something which is evident even now? The Queen even met Wajid Ali Shah's mother despite much opposition.

Statues of such an India-loving monarch should, therefore, not be dumped here and there but preserved to commemorate a part of our history which cannot be wished away. Delhi has shown the way with Coronation Park and other cities can follow suit. After all the Mughals too had come from another country and made India their home and gave us a good part of our heritage, including the Taj Mahal. Do we tend to dump their memory likewise?

Kolkata is spending a great deal of money to renovate the Victoria Memorial, which happens to be one of the best historical sites of that city. Surely Agra can do the same. Hewett Park can remain Paliwal Park as a reminder of Edward VIII's Indian counterpart who renounced a powerful U.P. minsterial post to marry the Begum who had stolen his heart. Incidentally, the rationing system as we know it was first introduced by Shri Krishan Dutt Paliwal and it continues to this day while some of his descendents have become owners of parts of the buildings of the old Johns Mills in Jeoni Mandi on the Yamuna bank overlooking the Taj.

Where Old Meets New

Chandni Chowk's *galis* and *kuchas* harbour many a secret. Take Naiwara, to reach which one has to pass through narrow lanes criss-crossing each other in which two men can hardly walk abreast. It was in such *galis* that Nadir Shah's soldiers got caught after they were ordered to massacre the citizens of Delhi in 1739, from 9 am to 2 pm, when Mohammad Shah threw himself at Nadir's feet and begged for mercy:

> Delhi's streets are flowing with blood and every able-bodied person has been mortally wounded or has perished. If your wrath has not yet abated, you will have to put life back into the corpses that have piled up to renew the slaughter (Qatal-e-aam), oh mighty warlord

That sobered down Nadir Shah and he asked his Persian troops to put back their swords in their scabbards. However, during that *tandav nritya* (dance of death) places like Naiwara by and large, escaped the bloodbath as access to them was so very difficult. Moreover the constant barrage of missiles in the form of stones, iron utensils *chakkipat* (millstones) and boiling water and milk thrown from the high-rise buildings forced the rampaging soldiers to retreat and not venture deeper. Such a scenario was witnessed again more than 100 years later when the British made the final assault to recapture Delhi. Patni Mal ki Haveli is a landmark in Naiwara, which now houses Suraj Kanya Shikshalaya.

The first Suraj Kanya, presumably, was Surajmukhi, Prithviraj Chauhan's daughter, for whom the first storey of the Qutub Minar (later built upon by Qutubuddin Aibak and Iltutmish) is believed to have been erected, so that she could see the Yamuna at dawn and worship the sun. Now the 350-odd girls studying in this middle school are all considered 'Surya Kanyas' and are lavished such love and affection that they never think of leaving it till passing out.

Patni Mal was a wealthy merchant of Chandni Chowk whose two-storied, spacious mansion was later handed over to nearby Indraprastha Girls' School in 1924 by Lala Jagan Nath, for running its primary section. The school, reached through Chawari Bazaar Chowk via Nai Sarak and Chipiwara, still retains its old world charm, like the Rajasthani-style balcony and canopy above the main entrance in marble, with intricate designs, pillared rooms and arched verandahs.

Now after renovation it is a mixture of the old and new. The courtyard, where once purdah ladies danced and swung on rope *jhoolas* at the Teej festivals, or celebrated Janmasthami, Diwali (with a hundred earthen lamps) and Holi (when rainbow colours blotted out even the sunlight), is now the place where the students assemble in the morning to welcome the new day with a song before entering their classes.

And what unique classrooms they have: arched with exquisite *dalan*-type enclosures that breathe of the 19th century. In one of them was a well, a deep one, from which water was drawn before Delhi got its piped water supply. The cool water of the well was a blessing in the summer months, when there were no refrigerators. In the aftermath of the revolt of 1857, when a lot of wells in the city had been either poisoned or had corpses of the slain dumped into them, such mansions as this haveli were a real oasis for the thirsty as the wells were hidden inside the living rooms. Now since the wells have lost their utility, the one in an ante-room of the senior classes has been closed, says the principal, Manjula Sharma. She leads one through the classrooms and up a flight of stairs to the roof where too classes are held in newly-built rooms, with a wire meshing to keep out monkeys which are a real menace. Before the school came to be housed here, there were probably *kaua-haknis* (women who chased away crows) and men employed to scare monkeys. But now it's the meshing that keeps away these marauders.

Standing in the balcony one imagines the time when husbands hiding behind their big-Rajasthani-skirted wives watched the Persian soldiers looking for human fodder for their swords, which were drawn out when the huge one of Nadir Shah was unsheathed at Sonheri Masjid, near the erstwhile Kotwali, opposite the Fountain. 'So long as my sword is out of its scabbard, kill everyone you come across', were the invader's words. But now what one sees is a long queue of parents waiting for school to give over, so that they could escort their children back home in the nearby or far away *kuchas*.

'These are bad times', remarks 90-year-old Narain Prasad, president of the managing committee of Indraprastha Girls' School, the parent body of Suraj Kanya Shikshalaya, 'when even young girls run the risk of abduction or molestation. So no one wants to take chances.'

As one descends from the balcony through a narrow staircase, that also breathes of old times, one cannot shake off the feeling that after seeing the bloodbaths of 1739 and 1857, the inmates of this haveli (though some wonder if another one stood here then) must have hurriedly descended through it to take refuge from the killers who had been let loose in the city. Now, of course, it's the girls who run down this staircase to rush into the arms of their waiting parents.

Clio on a Sunny Afternoon

About 50 people from different professions, scientists, businessmen, a photographer, a history buff and housewives, all flocked to hear a talk on Delhi of the past, when Vikramjit Singh, who heads the Delhi Heritage Photography Club, held an interesting seession at the enclosure of Wazirpur ka Gumbad. They sat on the grassy lawn just outside a medieval *baoli* or step-well and did not let their attention waver despite the distraction caused by children.

Vikramjit's Namdhari sect had a 19th century guru, Ram Singh, who was exiled to Rangoon some years after Bahadur Shah Zafar, following the Kuka rebellion of 1872. That's how the young business executive got interested in history. Well Wazirpur ka Gumbad, despite a temple and a gurdwara on one side, is still very much a picturesque place.

Ramakrishna Puram has around it the villages of Munirka, Mohammadpur, Basantnagar and Kusumpur. The area is dotted with numerous tombs, mosques and pavilions, most of them of the Lodi period. Here we have the three-domed Tin Burji, east of Mohammadpur, Malik-Munirka Mosque in Munirka (Wazirpur ka

Gumbad is 1 km to its north) and the domeless Munda Gumbads nearby. Munirka Gumbad, south-west of R.K. Puram, has an octagonal chamber and Bada Lao ka Gumbad to its east. Bajre ka Gumbad, 500 metres away is on the north-east and a nameless tomb to the north-west dating to Sikandar Lodi's time. Another monument of the second Lodi ruler's time is Khwajasarai Basti's tomb, along with a beautiful *baoli* with *dalans* or verandahs.

To the west is a mosque with inscriptions of Quranic verses. Its gateway has a *chhatri* as its crown. The tomb of Basti Khwajasarai is in front of the gate. The Khwajasarais were hermophrodites who were born as such with underdeveloped male organs. Khwajasarai Basti served Sikander Lodi and was honoured by him even after death, as is evident from his monument.

In South Extension-part I, north of the Ring Road, is Kale Khan ka Gumbad built in 1481, at the time of Bahlul Lodi, founder of the dynasty. In it is buried Mubarak Khan, father of Darya Khan, whose tomb is near by. Not far away are the Bhure Khan ka Gumbad and Chhote and Bare Khan Gumbads.

Kotla Mubarkpur has the tomb of Mubarak Shah Sayyid who reigned from 1421 to 1434. He was murdered at the time of Friday afternoon prayers at the behest of Sarvur-ul-Mulk whom he had dismissed as revenue minister. 'With a low dome, buttresses and *chhatris*, the tomb looks stunted but is a good example of the octagonal Sayyid tombs', says Dr Y.D Sharma

When Delhi was planned by Shahjahan, it had Agra as its model. Whatever embellished the capital of Akbar, Jahangir and Shahjahan initially reintroduced in Shahajahanabad, and whatever was dross was omitted. The narrow streets of the older city were a hindrance to the smooth flow of traffic. They also got choked when royal processions were taken out. The shops that came up in Chandni Chowk and the *mohallas* surrounding the Jama Masjid were low compared to the ones in Agra, where few of these survive. During the time of Jahandar Shah (1711-12), the dandy emperor's detractors used to refer to Chandni Chowk as Kothawali ka Rasta because his concubine, Lal Kanwar came that way to the Red Fort.

In Mohammad Shah Rangila's reign it acquired the epithet of Rangila Chowk but in 1739, when Nadir Shah massacred the residents, it was branded as Khooni Chowk. To the north of it the Red Fort square is cluttered up with all sorts of vehicles now but there was a time when mud houses made this place a veritable *jhuggi-jhonpri* colony. That was after 1857 when Bahadur Shah had been banished to Rangoon, and the fort placed at the disposal of the British troops. People who had been uprooted during the uprising found shelter in mud hutments which led to the formation of slums right up to Kashmere Gate. Delhi has many *kuchas* or enclosed localities but Kucha Dilwali Singh (or Singhan) is one which has an enviable history. The personage who lent it his name was the *mamu* (maternal uncle) of Guru Govind Singh. The story is now the stuff of legends.

How did lonely people pass their time in Delhi? Now of course there are the movies, TV, recreation clubs, restaurants, parks, public lectures and the world of art. Marco Polo, a columnist who toured India 50 years ago, found to his disappointment that even after Independence the people had changed little from 1908 when Sir Frederick Treves remarked on them. Later, the novelist E.M. Forster had commented that loneliness affected more people in India than perhaps anywhere else in the world. To get over loneliness some still tell tales, like the fishermen of the Jama Masjid area. When the tales end it is time for the fishermen's dinner. But that Sunday it was time for the historiographer, Marris Akbarabadi Sahib to leave for a late lunch after his exhilarating narration.

Lament for the Burafkhana

The Burafkhana, in between Pul Bangash and the old *subzimandi*, has long ceased to function. But you may still find some dealers selling ice round about the place, now littered with junk, but no manufacturers. The last nail in the coffin of this landmark ice-factory was driven, when the licence to local butchers for the export of mutton to West Asia was withdrawn by the government.

There was a slaughter house near by once, for which lots of ice was needed, and when it was moved to Qasabpura, the same practice of ice supply continued. Then the slaughter house shifted to Ghazipur, across the Yamuna and ice-making in the city ended altogether. The small supply in demand is brought from there, and in any case, many do not need it because of widespread use of refrigerators.

No one really knows when the Burafkhana came up. The guess is after the Revolt of 1857, towards the end of the 19th or at the beginning of the 20th century. The ice was needed by the British to cool their water and dinner drinks. The ice-pits of the Mughal period had stopped making ice during the Revolt and, since the icemakers did not resume manufacture, the sahibs were badly hit, along with the local population. As a matter of fact, the evening meal in the hot months could not be relished without iced water.

Ice sellers like Nadir and his brothers, big burly men who had been wrestlers, chiselled ice from huge blocks till late at night and kept many awake, including children who got over their fear of the dark and the discomfort of the sweaty night by just listening to the reassuring 'tick-ting, tick-ting' of the chisel and the cool thoughts it brought. How important ice was for a city like Delhi can be gauged from this quotation from Percival Spear's *Twilight of the Mughals*:

> The last solace of the English in the hot weather was ice. Down country none was available until 1833, when it was imported by ships from America as ballast. The captain of the first ship received a letter of gratitude from the Governor General. In Delhi the old Mughul custom of bringing ice from Srinagar in Garwhal by relays of runners (or in bullock carts) was too expensive for revival. It continued in Lahore for the supply of Ranjit Singh's Court. But the method of making ice in the cold weather by running water into shallow pans in the season of the cold winds and storing the ice in pits against the hot weather, was continued. Companies were formed whose members received ice regularly during the hot weather in proportion to the number of shares they held. The cutting off of the supply from the ice-pits was one of the hardships suffered by the garrison (British) during the siege of 1857.
>
> The ice-bed was divided into six-foot squares each about eighteen inches deep. In these were strewn straw of various kinds. Water-pots were provided for each square, and should the weather promise a cold clear night, water was poured into

cloth-bottomed pans which were then fitted into the earthen squares or hollows. On a good night ice would form to the depth of one and a half inches on the pans. This was gathered by shivering coolies in the early mornings and stored in ice-pits.

The pits were covered with a low mud house thickly thatched, drained by a well, and further protected from the air by layers of straw. The highest temperature at which ice could be made was about forty-three degrees (F); the pits were opened at the beginning of the hot weather and the supply lasted as late as August. Each night in December and January the old *abdar* would keep his watch. If the winds were fresh and likely to increase, he wrapped his blanket around him and retired to his bed, but if the air was clear and frosty, a drum was beaten and from the nearest bazaar came lines of muffled figures to fill the pans and fix them in the beds. The ice-beds were between the Delhi and Turkman Gates of the city and the icemakers lived in the village of Banskauli.

The Burafkhana took over from where the old icemakers had left—with machinery that could freeze water even in summer. Incidentally, the spot where the Burafkhana came up was once occupied by an Armenian church that was destroyed during Nadir Shah's invasion in 1739. Old habits die hard and even now boys from nearby areas come to the place with bags to buy ice from retailers, for cooling the capital's turbid water, especially during the breaking of the Ramzan fast. In summer the sellers spend the afternoon lying on the rag-covered ice blocks, kept under shady trees, perhaps dreaming of the times when their forefathers made ice in winter.

Believe it or not, one of them nearly married an amorous Englishwoman who was his favourite customer. Butcher Irshad Qureshi swears it's true because his grandfather told him so. That old timer in turn had heard the yarn from his grandfather. What's more, he disclosed that little pieces of ice were discreetly put in the *kurtis* (short shirts) of Red Fort harem inmates by fun-loving princes, out to tickle them into a romance. Can you imagine ice being made at Turkman Gate now and people falling in love in the process, not necessarily only on Valentine's Day?

Mughal Era Lingers on

Mughal culture has not totally disappeared from Delhi,' British scholar and historian, Dr Rosie Llewellyn Jones had remarked during one of her visits to Delhi. She thought it was something unique to the capital as most cities in Europe had put their past behind while embracing the new.

As if to bear out her statement, an exhibition on *Mughals: Life, Art and Culture* was inaugurated at the Indira Gandhi National Centre for the Arts in Janpath that very week—a facsimile of the acclaimed treatise it contained an extensive collection of illustrated manuscripts and paintings 'from scenes of courtly life, including lively hunting parties, and formal portraits of emperors, to illustrations of works of literature,' which have never been published before.

Among the exhibits were Shahjahan's recipe book, an 17th century manuscript—he was a great gourmet in his youth—*Notebook of Fragrance* (the Mughals had a large assortment of scents); *Book of Affairs of Love* by Rai Anand Ram Mukhlis (which has one illustration of Mohammad Shah Rangila making unconventional love), *Reminiscences of Imperial Delhi* by Sir Thomas Metcalfe (the Scottish nabob), with illustrations by the great painter Mazhar Ali Khan—a route map from Delhi to Qandahar (once part of the Mughal Empire), a riverfront map of Agra (when the Yamuna flowed near the Agra Fort) and a bird's-eye view of the Red Fort (a citadel that surpassed even the Camelot of King Arthur). Besides there were Mughal miniatures and the only portrait of Bahadur Shah Zafar taken by Capt. Robert Tytler and Charles Shepherd in 1858, as he lay ill on a stringed charpoy after the recapture of Delhi by the British, his hookah by his side.

But to go back to what Dr Rosie Jones said, a walk down Chandni Chowk will confirm that quite a lot of Mughal culture is still preserved as though by a wave of a fairy's wand. The shop from where Ghalib (1797–1869) bought his bottle of Old Tom, near the Fountain, may not be there, nor Faiz Nehar, but Ghantewala Halwai, established in 1790, whose sweets were savoured by Mughal emperors from Shah Alam to Zafar is still popular. Parantha Gali, where the descendants of the owners and their servants—all from the Chambal region who fought during the Uprising of 1857, alongside the rebel sepoys—ply their trade despite the challenge from fancy sari emporiums and still talk of the *Ghadar* as though it was a yesterday occurrence.

In fact, one milkman in the *gali* had a *lathi* in his shop, which was wielded by his great-grandfather in those days. The *sugandis* or perfumers stock the *attars* fancied by the Mughal begums from the days when Nur Jahan's m other, Asmat Begum discovered attar-e-gulab. The *chaat* and *kulfi* enjoyed by the *bankas*, the Dullissimo Macaroni of Delhi, who got the name from their slanted dandy walk, have not lost popularity either, despite the ice-cream craze.

The old *mohallas* of Daryaganj, behind Golcha Cinema also have not changed much. Tihraha Bairam Khan Road, where Sir Sayyid Ahmad Khan (1817–1898) lived before going to Aligarh (he returned to see the damage to his ancestral house after the so-called Mutiny) continues to have *bharbhooja* (gram roaster), *sabzi* and butcher shops as of old.

Zeenat Mahal (constructed in 1846) may be in a shambles but Hakim Ahsanullah Khan's haveli (built in 1730) and that of Lala Chunna Mal (built in 1848) are intact. The haveli of Zeenat Mahal—the third and most favourite wife of the last Mughal emperor, Bahadur Shah Zafar—at Lal Kuan in Old Delhi, which spreads over four acres, is a free-for-all ground for encroachers.

The haveli of Hakim Ahsanullah Khan—a personal physician of Bahadur Shah Zafar and a great friend of Mirza Ghalib—however, was built much earlier during reign of Emperor Mohammad Shah, near Mehrauli-Badarpur. Reduced to half and less attractive, it is fortunately deemed as a protected site by the Government that still requires rework.

The haveli of Chunna Mal—one of the wealthiest people in Delhi after the 1857 Indian Rebellion—situated in Katraneel region in the heart of Chandni Chowk, Old Delhi is probably one of the only havelis still preserved and inhabited by his descendants.

The old *sabeel* or waterhut at the entrance of Ballimaran, mentioned by Ahmad Ali in his *Twilight in Delhi*, is now fitted with taps for wayfarers to quench their thirst. Ballimaran more than 150 years ago was where the greatest masters of Urdu poetry, Mirza Ghalib lived. The bearded men of his time, who poured out water from long-stemmed *lotas* are long dead. But some *sakkas* or water-carriers, whose forebears provided water to Mirs and

Mirzas, besides the hoi polloi, are still around in front of the Jama Masjid, jingling their cups as they did at Kashmere Gate, when the Mughal freedom-fighters badly needed water for drinking, or to wash their wounds, before the dying Brigadier-General Nicholson (1822–1857) did so.

The hoteliers of Matia Mahal claim to have Mughal recipies as an ancestor of Karim's had worked in the royal kitchen at the Red Fort, when Mirza Fakhru (1816–1856), Bahadur Shah Zafar's eldest son, distributed bread to the royal residents and acquired the sobriquet of Mirza Chappati. The descendants of Nabbu Mian, another cook from those times, serve *kakori kababs* at Al Kausar, which they claim are prepared according to the secret recipes left behind by him in 1896, and the kin of Maseeta, may still be found in new Mina Bazaar. Ghalib was very fond of *kababs* made by Maseeta, whose counterpart in Lucknow was Tunda. After the devastation of 1857, Ghalib wrote to a friend in Jaunpur that Shahjahanabad had become such a despicable place that dogs growled about in Maseeta's shop (below the steps of the Jama Masjid), as the *kababia* had stopped using it for fear of the avenging British.

The walls of Kashmere Gate are pockmarked of the British cannonading and the remaining skeletal part of the Delhi Gate wall continues to have the sentry tower set up during Shah Alam's reign in 1804, when Colonel Ochterlony (1758–1825), defended the Walled City from the attacking Marathas of Yashwant or Jaswant Rao Holkar (1776–1811), who wanted to seize the emperor.

A *phuwara* came up on the spot where the bodies of Mughal princes shot by Hodson (1821–1858) lay for days, now part of Bhai Mati Das Chowk evoking strong memories. Lt Hodson's most celebrated action in British 19th century annals, was to apprehend the emperor of Delh. Though a few East India Company officials, felt the killing of Mughal princes by Hodson was not so honourable, he, however, received ample praise from others, including the Governor General. He met his nemesis during the British attack on Begum Kothi in 1858 when he was killed by a rebel sepoy.

Similarly, the place where Guru Tegh Bahadur met his end in 1675, when he was beheaded on the orders of Aurangzeb, is now part of Gurdwara Sis Ganj Sahib (built in 1930). The trunk of the tree under which the Guru was beheaded is preserved as is the well from which he took his bath while in the prison. Standing adjoining the gurdwara was the *kotwali* (police station), where the Guru and his disciplies were imprisoned and tortured. Now this too has become part of the gurdwara.

Wherever you go in these parts you cannot shake off the feeling that Mughal era life and culture lingers even in the 21st century

Majestic Memories

Majestic Cinema is long gone, having become part of Gurdwara Sis Ganj, but its memories remain. Atop the cinema used to be an idol of Lord Krishna playing the flute and at Janmashtami time people, who generally ignored it throughout the year, made it a point to venerate it. They did not go up to the high point where it stood but flocked near the Northbrook Fountain with joined hands to make their supplications. It was only after that that they went to the Gaurishankar temple to pay ritualistic homage while the dancing girls found their partners at the flower-sellers' stalls. Majestic came up in the beginning of the 20th century as a threatre (with an actors' gallery) at which the Parsi Theatre group was prominent among the performers. Once the *bhishtis* sold their *mashaqs* (water-skins) and the dhobis their bullocks to buy tickets for a show that was billed as the greatest at that time. Among the performers (if memory serves right) were Prithviraj Kapoor, Zohra Bai, Sohrab Modi and Mehtab. In those days the theatre groups used to come from Bombay and Calcutta to perform in the city which had just regained the status of the capital of the country. Chandni Chowk was the main business, religious, political and cultural centre and many of note lived in it.

During Janmashtami, after a visit to Jhandewalan temples, women and children particularly visited the *jhankis* or tableaux depicting the birth of Krishan Kanhiya. While making their way back home to the blowing of conch-shells, they did not forget to cast one last look at the idol that graced Majestic Cinema. Now few remember the flute player of Vrindavan perched on high and one often wonders whether the idol was saved or went down with the demolished Majestic façade?

Haji Zahur, who used to sit every evening at his hotel in Urdu Bazaar with equally old friends, 50 years ago, would relate incidents connected with Majestic Theatre. One of the dhobis who had sold his bullock to watch the big show was confronted by his wife with a donkey saying, 'From tomorrow you will have to take the clothes for washing to the Yamuna in a cart drawn by this *gadha*'. The dhobi, who was drunk, embraced the donkey and with tears asked it to get back the bullock. His wife burst out laughing, remarking, and 'two of a kind are trying to undo a blunder'. The dhobi, however, got back his bullock by repaying the money paid for it in instalments. On hearing this, Maulvi Sahib disclosed that a *bhishti* who had sold his *mashaq,* to hear Zohra Bai Ambalewale sing, was confronted by his father in Saqqa Gali, where the water-carriers lived, with the question: 'What will you earn and feed your family from tomorrow?' Bhishti Ramzani was so full or remorse that he bought a new waterskin after pawning his wife's ring. Arshad, a hotelier who was also a poet, wrote a poem on another theatre Bai and took it to her personally at Fort View Hotel in Chandni Chowk where the actors were staying. He got her framed picture in return. Arshad Sahib used to garland it until his infuriated second wife sold the picture to the *kabari* and got a severe beating for it.

Another friend of Haji Zahur, Ustad Zahooro went to meet his hero Sohrab Modi, one evening, and found him rehearsing at the hotel with young Mehtab. He had taken Ballimaran's *shammi kababs* and *roomali roti* with him. The actor was pleased with the gift no doubt, as he was a great gourmet and invited the ustad to attend a free show in the first class the next day. Thus did Delhi continue to be excited about the Theatrewallahs until they went back and sanity returned to the city. However, when the theatre became a cinema house it was youngsters like Ahmad Ali's character Asghar who defied family elders to watch late night shows. While returning from one of them, a barber named Kaley saw a ghost (sic) under the street-lamp in his *gali* and started getting epileptic fits until he was cured by an exorcist of Matia Mahal. But perhaps the most romantic incident is about Robin Haldar seeing a girl at the evening show, falling in love and finally marrying her. Their son went on to become an actor. Such are the memories of Majestic days that still enliven the evenings in some Old Delhi homes, more so at Janmashtami time.

Heritage of Mughal Clerics

The Shahi Imam of Jama Masjid, Syed Ahmed Bukhari, belongs to one of the oldest families of Delhi. His grandfather, Imam Abdullah Hamid Bukhari was regarded as a non-controversial cleric until he had a big tiff with General Shahnawaz Khan of Netaji's Indian National Army.

The General—who faced court martial, along with two other INA officers in Red Fort and was defended, among others, by Jawaharlal Nehru—had opposed the appointment of Abdullah Bukhari as the next Imam, contending that the decision rested with the Waqf Board and claiming the support of Barrister Nuruddin Ahmed.

Abdullah Bukhari did eventually succeeded his father and was once arrested for leading an agitation. One remembers him as an obese, fair-complexioned man, who had studied in St. Columba's School; however, looking at him one found it difficult to believe that. He would walk down from his spacious house in *gali* Imam Wali, fifty years ago, to lead namaz at the Jama Masjid, accompanied by a hefty, head-shaven, barefoot man, carrying a *lathi* and dressed in *kurta-tehmet*. It was Ahmed who kept looking to the left and right and keeping people away while the Imam, wearing dark glasses and a skull-cap above his long shirt and pyjamas, walked nonchalantly, with slow, heavy steps, acknowledging greetings from acquaintances.

A frowning Mir Mushtaq Ahmed (later Chief Executive Councillor of Delhi) looked down from his balcony in Urdu Bazaar. It was an open secret that he and the Imam were not on the best of terms. M.O. Farooqui, the Communist leader who lived close by, was an unconcerned observer, like Mustehasan Farouqi, caretaker of the shrine of Hazrat Kalimullah. But Imdad Sabri and area councillor, Chaudhuri Abdul Sattar had strong contrary views on the matter. Another ambivalent balcony looker on was Haji Zahooruddin of Haji Hotel, bang opposite the masjid.

Abdullah Bukhari had a powerful voice which could be heard as far away as Daryaganj at the two Eids, and specially the last friday of Ramzan, when the Mewatis and others came from Haryana to offer Alvida namaz in Edward Park, where they generally congregated.

The Imam began to be guarded after a man tried to attack him in Urdu Bazaar. When he became old and ill the question of his succession again led to a controversy, with some free-thinking Muslims questioning the right of the incumbent Imam to name his successor. But he had his way all the same and his elder son, Syed Ahmed Bukhari was appointed the next Imam.

One thing about Imam Abdullah Bukhari that few people knew was that he could speak and write good enough English and once surprised a British dignitary by interrupting the interpreter and answering a question himself—obviously the result of his early education. When the Imam of Kaba came to Delhi on a visit as guest of the Government of India, he was pleasantly surprised to find that the Imam could converse with him in Arabic directly. A Persian cleric was delighted when he briefly spoke to him in Farsi. Despite his flaring nostrils—usually associated with anger—he was not a quick-tempered man. He bore a strong resemblance to the colourful King Farouq of Egypt, though their tastes differed.

The Shahi Imam is a direct descendant of the first royal prelate of the Jama Masjid appointed by Shahjahan the 17th century. Syed Ahmed Bukhari has inherited the same outlook as his forebears and is looked upon by some as the repository of Islamic ideals. Incidentally, the names of all the Imams up to now are inscribed on a tablet in the mosque.

Historical Sites Through Tears

How many people weep when they visit Humayun's Tomb, which is the last resting place of several royals of the House of Taimur, or for that matter in the precincts of the Dargah Qutubuddin Bakhtiyar Kaki, where too Mughal kings and princes are buried? One does not know of any, except perhaps Bahadur Shah Zafar who sought safety at the tomb of his ancestor in 1857.

Be that as it may, Sharon Stone, the Hollywood actress, made history recently by becoming the first celebrity in recent times to weep over the graves of Shahjahan and Mumtaz Mahal, much as the royal couple's daughters must have done long ago. Jahanara and Roshanara probably did it out of a deep sense of personal loss, but Sharon was overwhelmed by the love story that gave birth to the Taj Mahal (described as 'a tear-drop on the face of Time').

Wiping her eyes, she came out of the cenotaph chamber after hearing the famous echo raised by the Khadim, to view the Yamuna and watch it meandering on to join the Sangam at Allahabad. But what made her weep again was the sight of the body of an infant being pushed about by a giant tortoise in the turbid water and some people defecating on the other side of the river. Delhi's Nigambodh Ghat too is not devoid of such scenes. No wonder she commented that a visit to India was 'both sweet and sorrowful'.

Alduous Huxley and T.S. Eliot were not exactly forthcoming in their praise of the Taj, but Queen Soraya liked it very much when she came with the Shah of Iran and also visited Fatehpur Sikri to seek in tears, the blessings of Sheikh Salim Chisti, so that she could bear a son and heir. But her wish remained unfulfilled and she was divorced not long after. Prince Akihito and Princess Michiko, as the Japanese crown prince and his consort, visited both the Taj and Humayun's Tomb, with the later-to-be Maharaja of Jaipur, Lt-Col Bhawani Singh, escorting them as military attaché to President Rajendra Prasad. In the 53 years after the imperial couple's first official trip, they visited India again in 2013 as the emperor and empress of Japan to revive memories, but they were past the age when they could become over-emotional. Even Princess Diana, who visited the Taj alone, as Prince Charles was supposedly busy elsewhere, did not weep inside the cenotaph chamber. Her eyes became moist only when she sat on the exalted marble seat above the lotus pond as she felt lonely without her husband, at a spot where couples flaunt their affection in accordance with the conjugal love symbolised by the Taj.

Jahanara's Tomb at Nizamuddin Dargah, partly of mud as per her wishes, and the more grandiose one of Roshanara in the garden named after her, do not generally have visitors shedding tears. The two died as spinsters, though both are said to have had affairs, which did not consummate in marriage because of the Mughal tradition of warding off contenders to the throne from the female line. However, if oral history is to be believed, a dying poet who had fallen in love with Jahanara (defying the adage '*par kartarney ko kainchian lagi hain dewar par*', which means there are scissors on the walls to clip wings of lovers) had expressed the wish that his remains be re-interred near those of his lady-love, after she too expired. The poor dejected poet was too small a fry to have his wish granted by Aurangzeb who, in any case, did not like Jahanara and was closer to his confidante Roshanara. The latter, however, did not pine for any lover as she was not as tender-hearted as her elder sister. She was a noted poetess too.

One rememebers a young man called Yusuf Hussain, a little disoriented in a Sufi attire, reciting verses of mystic love at Jahanara's grave. He had been infatuated by her after watching the 1960s film *Jahanara* at the now closed Jagat Cinema, in Jama Masjid's Macchliwalan area. Handsome and eloquent, he was much sought after by the gay men of those days, who sometimes made life miserable for him. So much so he would run away to Nizamuddin, where he squatted at the humble tomb, put his head between his black lungi-drapped legs and wept his heart out as though seeking solace from the lovelorn princess. Well Yusuf is long dead. Some say that he was pushed into an overflowing nullah in Nizamuddin. Others claim he was stabbed by an infatuated poultry seller of Seelampur. Whatever may be the truth one misses him alright.

About Roshanara's tomb, near which the Roshanara Club came up in 1922 also there's a story. A British lieutenant who used to visit the club, spent some time weeping at the grave of the princess after having his drinks. Probably he had fallen in love with Roshanara (if the living could do so with the dead). The late Raj Chatterjee, who became a member of the club later, vouched that the story was true and that Lieutenant Sharpe had to be sent back home as a nervous wreck. But for Sharon Stone to be moved to tears by a *khadim*'s account of the royal romance is something unusual. Could it be that it reflected her state of mind after some recent emotional setback?

Incidentally, the Lady of the Taj is regarded as a patroness of women in distress. Even so let's savour Sharon's deeply heaved sigh that mingled with tears to become a sonorous echo in the high-vaulted dome of the edifice of eternal love. Some say the Aga Khan looked as deeply moved after his Trust's renovation of Humayun's Tomb.

Feasts and Festivals

Ah, my beloved, fill the cup that clears
Today of past regrets and future fears
Tomorrow, why tomorrow I may be
Myself with yesterday's sev'n thousand years
Omar Khayyam

Flying Nostalgia on a Kite

Independence Day, Rakshabandan, Sankarat and Republic Day witness renewed interest in kites and even grown-ups, including the white-collar ones, are not averse to trying their hand at a tangle in the skies. There was a time when Basant was also among the kite-flying days, the main venues being the shrine of Hazrat Turkman Bayabani and later the grounds of Bhuli Bhartiyari ka Mahal, on the Karol Bagh Ridge (where *patang manja* or kite string too was made). But now one only sees yellow kites being flown at the Yogmaya Mandir, to gauge the weather until Holi.

However, Lahore is also known for its Basant kite festival despite a government ban on the popular celebration. A welcome change is the introduction of huge weird-shaped Chinese, Japanese and European kites at competitions, in places like Gujarat, Rajasthan and Delhi, whose biggest kite market is in Sadar Bazaar. Incidentally, Ghalib in his boyhood flew kites at Agra's Kala Mahal, along with Raja Chait Singh's son.

Eighty-year-old Bhai Mian is now regarded as the oldest kite-flyer (*patangbaz*) of Delhi, but he only took to the sport seriously in 1970 at the age of 37. Before him also there were expert kite-flyers, among them the sons of Shah Alam, Akbar Shah and Bahadur Shah Zafar. One of the Shah Alam's temporary successors even lost his kingdom for being tempted to fly a *patang* outside the Red Fort rather than attending to his newly-assigned duties by the invading Rohillas. Before Partition some of the noted *patangbaz* (not to mention those who flew kites to send messages to their girlfriends) were Langra Hafiz, Mullah Nadir, one-armed Kabir, Salim Habashi, Manu gambler, Razak Jebkat (pickpocket), civet-faced Biju and strongman Shahabuddin, who could also twirl a *lathi* alongside Phoonsi Khan.

This diminutive street-hector, as his name indicates, was a distant relation of Munshi Abdul Karim, Queen Victoria's Urdu teacher. Phoonsi Khan would tie a *tawa* (hotplate) on his head and armed with a *lathi*, fight with rival ruffian gangs for wangled money when not passing the evening in flying kites on the roof of his ancestral house in Deori Begum locality. Came 1947, and he migrated to Karachi and the police heaved a sigh of relief. Manu once won a fortune at cards, along with Salim, which made him change his attire to silk shirt and trousers. But Salim continued to wear his *pyjama-kameez* and stay in a discarded *astabal* (stable), decorated with kites, which he flew from nawab sahib's *kothi*. He was supposed to be hawk-eyed, which made him win many bets, a trait he could not pass on to his gay teenaged friend Lachoo. One-eyed Razak once tried to cut the boy's neck with razor-edged *manja,* but the *patang* got entangled in his shirt collar, which got sliced off like a mellon-piece.

Mullah Nadir sold his *thhela* (cart) to participate in a kite competition in Bareilly and Langra Hafiz was said to have wagered his young wife at a *patang*-flying contest. Luckily he won, but his wife divorced him all the same and returned to her parental home in Rampur with her two little children. As for Ustad Shahabuddin, Partition meant the end of his *ustadi* days in Tihraha Bairam Khan, from where he often rode on a bicycle with an iron rod tied to it, just in case some jealous *patangbaz* attacked him on the way to the Jama Masjid, where his favourite kite shop was situated and where he courted the company of good-looking boys. The most attractive of them was Iqbal Bhai, who went along with him to Lahore, where he began to participate in Basant kite-flying.

Now for the history of *patangbazi*: Kites may have been invented by Archytas of Tarentium in 4 BC and known to the Maoris since times immemorial, yet the art of kite-flying found its fullest expression in India—with Delhi being the main centre.

True, we might not have the singing kites of the South Seas, nor the ritual kite songs which warded off evil spirits. But the singing part of the kite was probably due to the special reed employed—good or bad. Good, clean kite-flying was what Delhi was famous for. There were no rituals or charms attached to the art, but just the sport. And here came in the question of kite-flying or tangles. Nowhere else did it reach the zenith that it did in the Capital.

Came Partition and Delhi lost a good many of its traits and with them some of the arts it was famous for. The Mughals had nurtured kite-flying with great care and mastered it towards the decadent years of their empire. A nephew of Bahadur Shah Zafar, who lived to be ninety, is supposed to have been the greatest kite-flyer of Delhi. Whatever little property was left to him by the British was sold bit by bit to buy kites and fly them in the competitions held then in Delhi, Lucknow, Bareilly and Agra. Mir Sahib, as he was known (no one seems to remember his real name), became a pauper and the residents of Matia Mahal, in the Jama Masjid area, had to raise funds to help the prince open a shop. Of course, he sold kites at his shop and, more often than not, gave them free to urchins whose love for the sport he encouraged. They nicknamed him Mir Patang, and he enjoyed that title for the rest of his life.

Qawwalis at 'Giant's' Grave

About 1.5 km north of Majnu ka Tila is the giant grave of a Naugaza Pir. Of late, qawwalis are held near the nine-yard-long tomb of the saint.

Nobody seems to know what his name was but some claim that it was Abdullah Nasir Shah Tilawaley or Syed Ibrahim Badshah. Some believe he had been a disciple of Majnu, who he rebelled against when he became a follower of Guru Nanak in 1505. This Majnu, unlike the one who wasted away for his beloved and gave birth to Nizami's masterpiece, *Alif-Laila*, was not a disheartened lover but one lost in devotion to God. When Guru Nanak visited, Majnu is said to have realised that he had met his true guide. A historic gurdwara built later, and visited by other Sikh gurus, now marks the site.

Another belief is that he was a disciple of Shah Alam, a venerated pir of Firoz Shah Tughlaq's time (1351–1388), which is probably more correct as in Wazirabad where this mazar is situated one finds many historical monuments from Firoz Shah Tughlaq's time

Tibetans have started living around Majnu ka Tila, making it a virtual Tibetan colony, complete with eating houses that attract a lot of customers. Side by side have come up *akharas* (wrestling pits) where *pehalwans* grapple after rubbing mustard oil and *akhara* soil on their muscular bodies.

There's a ghat (stepped embankment) just north of Wazirabad village, which is actually a cluster of temples, old and new. Here Brahma, supposedly, did penance to bring back to memory the Vedas whose knowledge had forsaken him. It is called *nigam bodh* because of that. It has a temple believed to date back to Mahabharat times, where the Kauravas and Pandavas worshipped. This is also supposed to be the place with the oldest burning ghats. From there one can look back towards the rear walls of the Red Fort, close to which the Yamuna flowed before changing its course.

As is the trend these days, anonymous mosques and tombs are being increasingly adopted by those who have started calling themselves *sajjada nashins* or hereditary caretakers. Offerings made amount to a lot every Jumairat (Thursday) and fill up their coffers. In course of time, boundary walls come up around hitherto neglected graves, which are renovated and dubbed old miraculous Sufi mazars. Such seems to be the case with the grave of the Naugaza Pir.

Dr Khaliq Anjum, who has written a history of Delhi's monuments in Urdu, is also of the opinion that the said mazar has begun to be venerated because of tall tales and gossip, exploited by opportunists.

Naugaza Pirs, whose graves are found all over north India, right up to Kashmir, were not giants but their mazars are large as they were buried along with the green flag-bearing staff they carried. As time went by their stature, as measured by their last resting place, began to draw awe and wonder.

However, for those interested in qawwalis, the mazar of the Naugaza Pir is a new attraction. On Thursdays, a big crowd collects and the zeal of those gathered is to be seen to be believed, with some going into a trance or *hal*. Among them are women too.

Remember that Queen Victoria almost reached that state when a group of *qawwals* performed in 19th century England, courtesy her Urdu teacher, Munshi Abdul Karim. Others also who heard the singers at Buckingham Palace became ecstatic, without understanding a word of what was being sung. You may luckily see the same effect at the pir's grave.

Phoolwalon Ki Sair

The flower sellers who enact their annual part at the Phoolwalon ki Sair every September–October includes the great-great-great grandchildren of those who took part in the first festival 200 years ago. This is not surprising since generations in the Walled City have been continuing in the same profession as their ancestors. The silver leaf beaters of Ballimaran, the *kabab* sellers, the pulao, biryani and *sheermal* makers of Matia Mahal are some examples.

This festival, unique to Delhi, owes its origin to an incident in the Red Fort in the second decade of the 19th century. Mirza Jahangir, favourite son of Akbar Shah II, was denied the right to be his successor in preference to his elder brother Abul Zafar (who later came to be known as Bahadur Shah Zafar).

One day, when the British Resident at the court went to meet Akbar Shah, the topic of succession came up again, but the Resident (Charles Seton) stated the East India Company's known position very firmly. Angry at this Mirza Jahangir fired at Seton just as he was leaving the Red Fort, but missed. Seton turned his horse back and asked the prince to apologise, but he refused and taunted him instead by shouting *'Lu, lu hai bey'* (cranky booby, fie on you). The Resident then went back and returned with a whole posse of British troops, bent on avenging the insult. The prince was arrested and sent in exile to Allahabad in the year 1812.

His mother, Queen Mumtaz Mahal Begum, pined for him and vowed that if he were to return she would offer a chadar and floral *pankha* at the shrine of Hazrat Qutubuddin Bakhtiar Kaki and a canopy at the Yogmaya Mandir close by. As things turned out, her wish came true. Mirza Jahangir was sent back to Delhi after the British relented and there were grand celebrations, with drummers and *shehnai* players carrying floral and embroided *pankhas* to the mazar and temple in Mehrauli.

Since then, the festival has been observed as a symbol of communal harmony, except for brief periods during and after the Mutiny of 1857, and then again in the 1940s, right up to the partition. Jawaharlal Nehru revived the festival at the instance of Yogeshwar Dayal in 1961, and so it continues, with many states taking part. Interestingly, the first *pankha* made by the women of the *salatin* (poor ladies' quarters), in the Red Fort, was kept in the Diwani-i-Khas as per the queen's wishes).

Mirza Jahangir's behaviour on his return to Delhi worsened, and Akbar Shah agreed with the British (after he tried to poison his elder brother twice) that he be sent back to Allahabad. There he whiled away his time in drinking Hoffmann's cherry brandy and making merry with dancing girls. In 1816, Colonel Sleeman (who suppressed the Thugs) found him in a bad state. 'To obtain an interview with the Gov-Gen Lord Hastings, he promised to limit himself to one bottle of port wine daily,' according to Percival Spear.

Lord Hastings described him as wearing a Tartar dress, a crimson robe, blue vest, lined with fur and a high conical cap ornamented with fur and jewels, though it was the peak of summer. He had long hair, cut at the side—a handsome young man gone astray. The prince died in 1821, long before his parents, and was buried in a beautiful tomb in Delhi. His case was reminiscent of Absalom, King David's favourite son, who died as a tragic biblical figure over 3000 years ago.

Phoolwalon ki Sair wends its way through Mehrauli to the fountain led by *shehnai* players in brocade sherwanis and then to

Jahaz Mahal. This Mahal is shaped like a ship, hence its name. Bahadur Shah Zafar, who was considered gay by his father and so 'not worthy to be his successor' used to preside over the festival with great aplomb till 1856.

Despite all the fanfare that surrounds the festival, one thing that seems like a forgetful omission is that no one makes any offerings at the grave of Mirza Jahangir, whose exile started the hoary tradition. Sadly, the mausoleum of the colourful prince in Nizamuddin stays bereft of the homage due to him and to his mother.

Idgah Buzz Beyond Eid

To visit the imposing medieval Idgah, at any time of the year, is to be reminded of Id, whether Eid-ul-Fitr or Eid-uz-Zuha, which is now generally referred to as Eid-al-Adha.

Built during the reign of Aurangzeb (1658–1707), its erection was considered necessary by the emperor because of the existence of Akbar's Idgah in Fatehpur Sikri and the Idgah in Agra, which Shahjahan had built in 40 days and where he too in his younger days had offered namaz. Strangely enough it was located in the middle of a village in Namnair. The poor residents, deprived of toilets at home, used its unpaved courtyard as an open-air latrine. It was only during the two Eids that the mess was cleared.

Aurangzeb was naturally aware of this problem, so it was with great care that the site for the Delhi Idgah was selected on a part of the Ridge, which then did not have habitation close enough to pollute it. At Agra up to 1947, Nawab F.K. Sherwani continued to offer namaz, along with his sons, Turkish protegés and African retainers, after getting the Idgah courtyard cleaned three days in advance. The refuse however, still accumulates there.

Delhi's growing population saw new localities like Qasabpura, Bara Tooti and Bara Hindu Rao. They came up on one side of the Idgah and the poor quarter of Karol Bagh on the other. Bara Hindu Rao owed its inception to the brother-in-law of Daulat Rao Scindia, whose wife, Baiza Bai was the sister of Hindu Rao Ghatke, a man of great ambition and tact. The Gwalior ruler became wary of him and hit upon the idea of sending him to Delhi as his *eelchi* or agent. He was instructed to keep Scindia informed of the happenings at the Mughal court and the machinations of the British.

Hindu Rao managed to charm both and in the process won their confidence. He was a favourite guest at Gora Sahib parties (whose women lavished affection on him as he was in the habit of giving costly presents). A short, pauncy man with twinkling eyes, who wore pearl earrings, the Rao was also befriended by Bahadur Shah Zafar and his nobles and those in charge of the Idgah. No wonder he was present at the Eid celebrations there too. It was however, only after the murder of his friend William Fraser that he bought the late British Resident's mansion and added his name to it and to the sprawling locality nearby. Posterity later named a hospital after him.

It is recorded that Zafar, too old and feeble to visit the Idgah, was represented by his sons at it. After offering prayers in the Red Fort, the emperor waited for the princes to return and give him a vivid account of the size of the congregation, the sermon of the Imam and other happenings, like the mood of the people (whether hostile or conciliatory to the monarchy). This was necessary to ascertain because of the growing British influence in the city.

After the Revolt of 1857, Eid gatherings at the Idgah were discontinued for some time and later (on popular demand) allowed under strict watch. However, it was only in 1867 that a full-fledged Eid gathering was witnessed, presided over by Mirza Elahi Bux, the badshah's kinsman and the most noted surviving Mughal prince (besides the disabled Mirza Chingezi), after the death of Bahadur Shah and the elimination of his elder sons and a grandson.

The apple of Zafar's eyes, Jawan Bakht and his mother, Zeenat Mahal, however, continued to languish in exile in Rangoon. The Jama Masjid and Fatehpuri Masjid were under firangi control, though the latter was still in the possession of Lala Chunna Mal, whose hold was relinquished only in 1877. But the Idgah was free for worship as a British gesture of sorts. Later Elahi Bux's sons, Prince Sulaiman Jah (founder of the Anglo-Arabic School), and the ever-handsome Prince Soraya Jah, were prominent among the VIPs who offered namaz there and sacrificed goats or sheep at Bakr Eid. Some of them rest in the surrounding graveyard.

In the first decade of the 20th century, when both the Jah brothers were alive, as also their father, the nationalist wave and the agitation for the revocation of house tax saw the Idgah emerging as a favourite public platform. Historian Narayani Menon observes in her treatise, *Delhi Between Two Empires* thus:

> The use of the Idgah as a venue for a meeting in 1910 had a dual significance—it symbolised the growth of the western suburbs (of Delhi), with the Idgah a more accessible rallying point than the Jama Masjid. It also indicated the growth of politicisation, the opposition of the nationalist Muslims to the loyalist (of the British) *rais* or elite who controlled the Jama Masjid.

The importance of the Idgah, besides the Eid gatherings, can be gauged from the fact that it is the venue for multitudinous *itjima* and *tabliq* congregations that converge on its rocky eminence. Hence, it never lies neglected, the yearlong.

Qurban Ali's Sacrifice

During the last years of his reign, Bahadur Shah Zafar had imposed a complete ban on cow slaughter in keeping with the tradition set by his ancestor, Akbar the Great. The order may have been flouted in the villages round about but in the year preceding the Great Revolt the ban was strictly enforced in the urban area to strengthen communal harmony.

Zafar may have heard rumours about the gathering storm that was to strike North India but his subjects knew more about it even before the lotus and the chappati began to make their rounds, over hundreds of miles. It was Hakim Ahsanullah Khan who had cautioned the emperor that things were not as calm as they appeared '*Fiza kharab hai*' were supposed to be the actual words, according to Munshi Turab Ali an influential cleric of thse times. His kinsman Maulvi Rajab Ali was maligned following the murder of the emperor's sons and grandson by Lt William Hodson, who claimed to have got wind of Zafar's presence at Humayun's Tomb on

21 September 1857, through him. The descendants of the maulvi and munshi, however, refute this vehemently.

When the British regained control over Delhi they were told by their spies during the Bakri Eid, 158 years ago (when Zafar was being sent into exile) that though the prominent Muslim families had been banished from the city, the rural areas, where they had found shelter, were still seething with unrest and that it would be better if only sheep and goat slaughter was allowed to prevent communal clashes which may have repercussion in Delhi proper where the big Hindu families had been allowed to remain.

Ghalib, says Dr Narayani Gupta, lamented that upto 1869 there were mostly Hindu *sahukars* and the Muslim merchants who could be compared to them were not more than three. Bakri Eid was not as gay as it used to be although the Parsi and other shops were well stocked. The main celebrations were, according to contemporary accounts, limited to areas like Nizamuddin, Qutub Minar and Purana Quila. The Punjabi Muslim Katra, demolished to make way for the railway station, was virtually relocated in Kishenganj. However, considering that the trade in hides and skins was still centred in Delhi it is quite feasible that enough animals were being slaughtered once again.

Lala Chunna Mal was the wealthiest merchant, but his riches mostly came from the piecegoods business. At least this is what the controversial Bholanath Chunder made widely known, even though it was more of a generalisation than a fact.

It was about that time that Qurban Ali, a Punjabi Muslim merchant approached the Khatri Lala Chunna Mal with the request to relinquish control of Fatehpuri Masjid so that Bakri Eid could be celebrated with joy once again. Chunna Mal took an assurance from him that there would be no slaughter of cows. Qurban Ali, with great bravado, promised that it would be so though the butchers who had a side business in big hides told him in no uncertain terms that such a promise would hit their business. Thereupon, Qurban Ali gave his word of honour that he would compensate them for the loss they might suffer. This was taken with the proverbial pinch of salt by the butchers, but Qurban Ali kept his word though he suffered a big financial setback in the process. Chunna Mal gave up possession of the mosque and Eid namaz was held in it again in 1877.

However, Qurban Ali did not survive long after that and died of the shock that the slump in his business and the taunts of his wives and many children gave him. Qurban Ali's sacrifice is part of oral history and there are no records to substantiate it. But many in the Walled City up to 50 years ago swore that he had lived up to his name, for *qurban* means sacrifice. In the mid-1880s when there was intense Hindu-Muslim rivalry, culminating in clashes before Bakri Eid, the Tarwala Eid-Milan mela in Kishan Dass Gurwala's *bagh* was discontinued but resumed when peace between the two communities was restored.

One more thing associated with Bakri Eid or Eid-ul-Zuha (now more popular as Eid-al-Ada) was that most of the *qurbanis* performed were on the hilly area, surrounding the Idgah built in Aurangzeb's reign. Some are still carried out there, but Qurban Ali's soul must be resting in peace now that no cows are slaughtered in the capital. Even for goat and sheep sacrifice, policemen take an inventory by making a house-to-house check. Ironically, Lala Chunna Mal's name survives while that of Qurban Ali's is almost forgotten.

Diwali's Mughal Connection

The Rang Mahal in the Red Fort has been renovated and now the sagging ceiling of the Diwani-e-Khas is being set right by the ASI, not an easy task as the slightest miscalculation or deviation in laying the sal-wood planks can mar the symmetrical setting of the once gold-plated covering under the roof of the Hall of Private Audience, where the Takht-e-Taus or Peacock Throne occupied pride of place.

Such care was not needed in the Rang Mahal which was the venue of Diwali and Basant celebrations during the time of Mohammad Shah (1720–1748). Holi however, was celebrated in the front lawns, while the Diwali diyas lent lustre to the mahal.

And that brings us to the point of the Mughal connection with Diwali, which actually began in the reign of Akbar at the Agra Fort and Fatehpur Sikri, where the palaces of Jodha Bai and Raja Birbal were also situated. Jahangir and Shahjahan had milder Diwali celebrations and Aurangzeb was content with receiving gifts from his Rajput generals like Raja Jaswant Singh of Jodhpur and Jai Singh I of Jaipur.

His grandson, Jahander Shah ruled for just about a year and celebrated his Diwali at Lahore with concubine Lal Kunwar. All the oil in the city is said to have been bought by the dandy emperor to light up the night but, exaggeration apart, there were enough Telis there to cater to the needs of the hoi polloi-and some of them were more than mere oil sellers, for the saying in Lahore as also in Delhi, was '*Parhhein Farsi aur bechein tel*' (Study Persian, and sell oil). Some of these men where intellectuals who had to resort to such lowly jobs because of the difficult circumstances.

Diwali was considered, even by the orthodox Muslims, a festival of natural joy of God's creation, though some of them had reservations about eating *kheel* which, incidentally, was mostly sold by Muslim *bharbhujas* or gram roasters. Besides the Rangila (colourful) Mohammad Shah, his predecessor Farrukhsiyar had ordered Diwali illuminations at the Delhi Gate he had built on the Agra-Delhi road.

The Sayyids of Barah, who had put him on the throne and some other puppets, including Mohammad Shah too, belonged to 12 villages in what is now UP and where Diwali was celebrated with great enthusiasm, by the Hindu and Muslim peasants. So they were not surprised at the emperor's unusual spectacle.

A special feature of the Mughal celebrations at Shabh-e-Barat and Diwali was the bursting of crackers close to the walls of the Red Fort under the supervision of the Mir Atish (Fireworks incharge) during successive emperors.

According to historian R. Nath, in an age when there were no matches, the permanent source of fire was Surajkrant.

> At noon of the day when the sun entered the 19th degree of Aries, and the heat was the maximum, the (royal) servants exposed the sun's rays to a round piece of shining stone (Surajkrant). A piece of cotton was then held near it, which caught fire from the heat of the stone. This celestial fire was preserved in a vessel called *Agingir* (fire-pot) and committed to the care of an officer.

The fire was used in the palace and renewed every year. Camphor candles called *kufuri-shama* were placed on 12 candlesticks of gold and silver to light up the palace as a daily ritual, Dr Nath asserts. This was obviously done on a grander scale at Diwali when the *Akash Diya* (the Light of the Sky) was lighted with greater pomp, placed atop a pole 40 yards high, supported by 16 ropes, and fed on several maunds of binaula (cotton-seed oil) to light up the durbar. Just imagine the huge lamp lighting up a Diwali night and casting its glow right up to Chandni Chowk where rich seths had their own lighting arrangements, with mustard oil diyas on every building. A giant-size statue of Tesu Raja and his wife Jhainji, symbolised by illuminated pots, was also taken out for immersion in the Yamuna.

However, the Diwali of 17 October 1762 turned out to be a bleak one, but that is another story...

The Eighth Horse of the Sun

The 1995 eclipse on 24 October (*The Eighth Horse of the Sun*, as depicted by M.F. Husain) had a parallel in the one observed on 17 October 1762, which also happened to be a Diwali day. But, unlike 1995, the festival then was not observed a day earlier. It however, turned out to be a bleak Diwali for the people of Punjab because of the invasion of Ahmed Shah Abdali.

The Sikhs, who had been routed at Ghalugara earlier, in February, gave battle to the invader near Amritsar, but the combatants dispersed when they saw the sun turn black. They did not know that it was a solar eclipse. Thinking that it was a heavenly sign of displeasure, the Sikhs went into hiding in a forest and Abdali and his troops moved on to Lahore. Something like that happened when the Medes and Lydians were fighting a battle on the banks of the Euphrates. Scared that the gods had disapproved of the battle by making the sun invisible, the rival forces hurriedly agreed to a truce. The Greek hero Ulysses had good luck during two eclipses some 3000 years ago, but not against the Spartans.

Not only Punjab, but also Delhi and the neighbouring areas had an uneasy Diwali 230 year ago because of the fear of Abdali's forces. A year earlier, on the fateful battlefield of Panipat the Maratha confederacy led by Sadashiva Rao Bhau and Viswas Rao, the Peshwa's son, had been routed by Abdali. Both the commanders were killed and their artillery expert Ibrahim, wounded along with Scindia. Many see the Third Battle of Panipat as a precursor to the effects of the eclipse the next year.

Ahmed Shah Abdali was the Afghan commander of the forces of Nadir Shah who had ransacked Delhi in 1739 during the reign of Mohammad Shah Rangila. After his return to Persia, Nadir Shah, drunk with power, had become a ruthless despot. His elite corps, the Qasilbashes, hatched a conspiracy and killed him in 1747 and Abdali was made king in his place.

His first act was to capture Afghanistan and then Punjab, where the Mughal governor was hardly a match for his forces. He was, however, defeated by Prince Ahmed in 1748. But after that he raided North India seven times, coming up to Delhi, Mathura and Agra. The provocation for Abdali's attack on Delhi in 1756 was the growing power of the Marathas and the Mughal wazir who had come together to kill the emperor, Azim ul Dowlah (a puppet ruler) and installed Prince Ali Gauhar as Shah Alam II on the throne of Delhi. Earlier the Marathas had ousted Abdali's commanders in Punjab and seized Lahore.

Abdali recognised Shah Alam as emperor of Hindustan, after the Third Battle of Panipat. But the emperor stayed on in eastern India until his defeat by the British in the Battle of Buxar. That same year, 1764, the Sikhs seized Lahore and slowly became masters of Punjab with the emergence of Ranjit Singh.

Shah Alam signed the Diwani of Bengal at Allahabad in 1765 and returned to Delhi. Twenty-three years later, he was blinded by the Rohilla chieftain Ghulam Qadir who was ultimately tortured and put to death by Mahadji Scindia.

Ghulam Qadir had risen to power after the death of the great Rohilla leader Hafiz Rahmat Khan who was defeated by the British at the Battle of Miran Katra on 23 April 1774. It was an unprovoked action, and had Hafiz, who died bravely, survived, the emperor perhaps, would have never been blinded.

This is the course Indian history took in the wake of the total eclipse of 1762. The eclipse proved beneficial to the Sikhs, and disastrous for Abdali, though his last invasion took place in 1767, good in parts for Shah Alam, auspicious for the British, not too good for Hyder Ali but lucky for Scindia whose sphere of influence increased until the arrival of Lord Lake in 1803.

That is how the believers see it. But somehow the story that the Sikhs and the forces of Ahmed Shah Abdali took fright on sighting the eclipse does not gel. Akbar the Great had watched an eclipse and bathed at the Brahma Sarovar in Kurukshetra 182 years earlier. Ahmed Shah Abdali, an experienced commander, and the warlike Sikhs were not so naive, especially after Raja Jai Singh had set up his Jantar Mantar (observatories), in North India. Maybe, Abdali thought it prudent to hasten to Lahore to quell a mutiny, which would have cut off his access to Afghanistan and left him stranded in the plains of the Punjab. Many of course must have heaved a sigh of relief and lit their diyas all right.

Diwali Before and After 1857

Diwali before the Uprising of 1857 was not such a glamorous affair as it has now become. The most noted family, and perhaps the oldest, according to the old gazetteer, was that of Lala Sri Kishan Das Gurwala, bankers to the Mughals. It came into prominence during the invasion of Ahmed Shah Abdali in 1732.

The name Gurwala, wholesale merchants of gur, owes its origin to Lala Radha Kishan. He had nine sons: Bahadur Singh, Zaokiram, Sheonath, Mokham Singh, Jagannath, Magniram, Kedarnath, Girdhari Lal and Khushal Rai (after whom the *kucha* in Chandni Chowk is a famous landmark and where St. Stephen's College was first established).

Diwali at the houses of the nine lalas was a celebration, which was talked about the whole year, with many anticipating what form it would take the next year. The diyas placed by them at their havelis had wicks burning in pure ghee (purer than what you can get now) at a time when there were no electric lights. People from far and near came to see the illuminations, particularly at the house of Khushal Rai (more prosperous than others in keeping with his name), and the fireworks display, which rivalled that of the Red Fort. Diwali was a festival, like Basant, that was celebrated by the Mughals since Akbar's time and even Aurangzeb was not averse to greeting his Rajput generals and their families on the occasion and receiving gifts and sweets from them. Mohammad Shah Rangila, his great grandson, crowned in Fatehpur Sikri, sat with his courtiers while dancing girls with earthenware lamps danced around fountains that sprayed coloured water and, if gossip is to be believed, one of them sprouting liquor which many a nobleman drank with cupped hands to please the dandy emperor, much to the chagrin of the orthodox mullahs who thought it a sacrilegious exercise under the influence of Iblis (the devil). Mohammad Shah died in 1748, but his son, Ahmad Shah was more puritanical, spending time at the mazars of saints.

The Diwali of 1857, a hundred years later, was a dull affair because of the large-scale mayhem by the avenging British after the recapture of Delhi prior to Dusshera. The stench of the bodies of those gibbeted in Chandni Chowk still polluted the atmosphere. The *nehar* or canal that flowed through the Chowk retained traces of the bodies of the sepoys thrown into them and the Lalas had only a mild celebration with a few diyas burning and Lakshmi puja being held privately in homes. The business of the *halwais*, who made sweetmeats, had slumped and those who used to come for the festival to make a fast buck from places near Delhi, stayed away because of the atmosphere of fear and intrigue.

The Muslim shoe merchants, spending money on illuminations and exchange of sweets with Hindu businessmen to welcome the festival of good luck in the coming year, were under a cloud of suspicion as the British branded their community as the main instigator of the 'rebellion' that had ousted them from the Mughal capital, for four months, and resulted in the killing of their men, women and children. So the 'Jutawalas' were hardly in a mood to join the celebrations in bleak Diwali. But after Fatehpuri Masjid was recovered from Lala Chunnal Mal who had got it in an auction for ₹39,650, and the tommies who had occupied the Jama Masjid along with native solders from Punjab had left, the mood changed and Diwali slowly began to assume its earlier colourful character. But long before that time the five sons of Lala Radha Krishan were dead without any issue. The sixth had one son, the seventh and eighth also had one each living. Khushal Rai's son, Mathura Das was father of Bakshiram whose son Ramji Das fathered Narain Das who in turn adopted Srikishna Das the head of the family about the seventh decade of the 19th century.

The family celebrations were still something to talk about but new Lalas had emerged. Among those the names of bankers like Bishambar Das, who had bought the baradari of a son of Shah Alam II, Pandit Jwala Nath, who purchased the haveli of Nawab Muzaffar Khan and Lala Hardhyan Singh (after whom a road is named in Karol Bagh) bought the haveli of Hamed Ali Khan. Lala Ram Chand, Lala Mehar Chand, Lala Sultan Singh (founder of Modern School, Barakhamba Road), Lala Ram Kishan Das, Lala Sri Ram of DCM, Lala Basheshar Nath and the Chandiwallahs were prominent. They were the ones who kept Diwali glowing in the aftermath of 1857. But in the poor pockets like Mori Gate, Farashkhana, Ajmeri Gate, Turkman Gate and Delhi Gate, the illuminations were subdued naturally because of acute poverty. But in Bazaar Sita Ram the Kahishta Saxenas and Kashmiri pandits, in Roshanpura the Mathurs, in north Ballimaran the Hindu traders held good Diwali celebrations. One would like to add the name of the Rev. B.R. Winter, in charge of St. Stephen's Church, Fatehpuri and of Mrs Winter, to the list of noted Diwali celebrants. This Winter family had a great impact on Delhi because of their social service and it was long after their death that Daphne du Maurier made the surname famous again with her overbearing character, Max de Winter and his late wife Rebecca, the tragic mistress of 'Manderley'. What a link-up with Diwali!

New Year's Eve with Josh

Spending New Year's Eve with the doyen of Urdu poetry, Josh Malihabadi, during his visit to the Capital, from where he had migrated to Lahore in the 1950s, will always be etched in my memory. It was on the last day of 1967 that a group of *shairs* accompanied Shabbir Hussain Khan Josh to Moti Mahal restaurant in Daryaganj from the Jama Masjid area, where he was staying in a hotel near Jagat Cinema (this scribe's abode for some years), on a visit to the capital from Pakistan, where he had reluctantly gone on the nagging of his wife and settled down in Lahore, much to the regret of his close friend Jawaharlal Nehru. He spent an hour at the restaurant as he had to attend another engagement but that hour was filled with a rare joie de vivre.

The mood of the evening was set by Sehba of Agra who recited his ghazals in a sing-song voice that evoked nostalgic memories of the pre-partition years. Next Afzal Sahib, who had hosted Josh during his entire stay in Delhi, rendered his *nazms* of love and longing in which woman was exalted to godhood. He explained this candidly by asserting, '*Maine tau aurat ko khuda mana hai*'.

A lady sitting on a nearby seat gave him a curious gaze, as though wondering what the heck he meant. A *shair* from Jaipur, Betaab gave vent to his feelings in verse that verged on the moral that wine, women and song alone did not sustain Urdu poetry as there were other things that mattered and needed to be highlighted. Josh nodded as he had himself veered away from old nuances that harped on the *bulbul*, the *bayaban*, the ill-starred lovers and the Kohkaf (Causacus).

Sikandar Dehlvi, a thin young man with a prominent Adam's apple and a high-pitched *tarranum* (singing recitation), presented his *Sufiana kalaam*. He was seen every day at the mazars of Hare Bhare, Sarmad and Hazrat Kalumullah reciting his compositions after the *Maghrib* (sunset) prayers. But few paid heed as most of those assembled were eager to hear the qawwalis after 8 pm.

Gulzar Dehlvi, a noted Kashmiri Urdu poet, did not come that day but Madhosh Sahib, professor at REI College, Dayalbagh, was there along with Maikash Akbarabadi. Madhosh was already tight when he came but did not slur his verse, which came out distinctly. Maikash, whose *takkhalus* (pseudonym) meant wine-bibber, had however, never tasted liquor in all his long life. His intoxication was with the wine of love-divine and his poetry reflected his Sufi thought, for Maikash was also a pir with a wide following, among whom were the dancing girls of Mewa Katra, who came every morning to get their children touched by him and get *tawiz* (amulets), for averting the evil eye.

Josh's younger brother was not a poet but a linguist and zamindar and had come from Malihabad (near Lucknow) specifically to meet him and his *bhabi* (sister-in-law) who had asked him to bring some saplings (for transplanting) from the home of the dussheri mango, for which his home town is still famous. Addressed as 'Khan Sahib' by one and all, he looked lost amidst tipsy *shairs* and missed his *hookah*, left behind at the hotel. But occasionally he would discreetly correct the *taffazul* (pronunciation) of some *shair*. He asked one where he was originally from, for he saw a Punjabi tang in his recitation. 'I have been living in Delhi for *unnatees saal* (29 years)', he replied. 'The word is not *unnatees* but *untees*', said Khan Sahib, 'which means one less than 30 in Arabic'. The *shair* looked crestfallen but Josh, overhearing the conversation, asked him not to take the correction to heart but treat it as a piece of advice from an elderly man.

After some more *shairs* had their say, Josh cleared his throat. He had already taken three large pegs of Scotch and nibbled at a roast chicken and was in the mood to recite in his majestic voice that showed the mastery of an ustad. *Jab Cheen ne angrai li* (When China yawned). It also showed his Leftist leanings. Not for nothing was he known as the Shair-e-Inquilab. His *kalaam* was a constant attack on hypocrisy and bigotry, which had made him unpopular with the orthodox gentry of Lahore. But he cared a fig. His verse on Sawan, the rainy season, with the onomatopoeic sound of thunder, elicited '*wah-wahs*'. Josh looked flushed and in a mood to oblige those requesting him to recite some of his earlier verses. One of them ended with the words:

> *Tor kar tauba nadamat tau hoti hai mujhe ai Josh*
> *Kya karoon niyat badal jati hai saghar dekh kar*
> (After breaking the vow not to drink, I feel a pang of guilt, but what to do, the urge on seeing the wine-cup is too hard to resist)

This was greeted with a chorus of *qayaam* and *muqqarar* (request for encore). Sure enough Josh obliged again and after that got up saying he had to go. A big-built man, he still looked the picture of a robust Pathan despite his age. '*Naya saal phir se aya hai/Mubarak ho, mubarak ho*', sang the hotel *qawwals*. Josh raised his hand in saluatation and exclaimed, '*Tumhe bhi bhai, mubarak ho*' (Happy

New Year to you too) and walked out with his brother and others following him, giving the impression as though Omar Khayyam was taking leave after greeting the year to come: 'Now the New Year reviving old desires/The thoughtful soul to solitude retires'. Josh did not retire to solitude but to a mushaira at Haveli Sadr Sadur, Matia Mahal, where Ghalib often greeted the coming year!

Sawans, Past and Present

The rainy month of Sawan now seems to reinforce the age-old saying, *Na Sawan hare/Na Bhadon sookhe* (Neither is Sawan green nor is Bhadon dry). Delhi has been starved for rain many times in the past too. There was a big famine in Shahjahan's reign when as a prince, in 1630–31, Aurangzeb had to provide relief to the parched Deccan.

Sher Shah, Akbar and Jahangir also had to cope with famines and earlier Mohammad bin Tughlak. Shah Alam II could not do much when Delhi suffered drought as he was virtually a puppet of the Marathas. Akbar Shah–II's reign saw the fields across the Yamuna drying up in the absence of good rains. Afterwards, Bahadur Shah Zafar, whose kingdom had shrunk to the Red Fort side of the river, pleaded his helplessness to woebegone farmers.

After the 1857 revolt also, scanty rainfall made a lot of peasants miserable in Delhi. However, the gazetteer for 1883–84 reported Sawan once again living up to its reputation. Like in the days when Akbar enjoyed it with his Rajput wives and Salim (Jahangir) with Anarkali under shady trees at Fatehpur Sikri, though Shahjahan toned down the revelry after Mumtaz's death and Aurangzeb's ardour cooled following the untimely demise of Hira Bai Zainabadi.

In late 19th century, the villages were green as green can be, the Jats of the countryside making merry with folk songs and dancing in the fields, much like in Bollywood films, sans of course fancifully dressed-women in blue saris and men in green clothes to merge with the verdant surroundings. The zamindars were happy (said one land revenue British official) and so were their tenants, the *ryots*.

It is pertinent to point out that no one was aware of the El Nino effect then and poor monsoons were attributed to either the sins of the ruler or the *praja* (subjects). If the monsoon failed the luckier farmers were employed in famine relief works. Awadh, Bengal and Hyderabad being the best examples.

According to Francois Bernier, writing about the time of Aurangzeb, the emperor was initially interested in the welfare of the peasants but in the latter part of his reign (due to war in the Deccan) their condition grew worse and many of them had to work as coolies and camp labourers while lawlessness increased and Sawan songs were lost in lamentations.

After Aurangzeb's death, the Marathas levied higher land tax. The excuse was that it was being fixed as at the time of Raja Todarmal in Akbar's reign or by Malik Ambar in Shahjahan's time. As the Mughal Empire declined agriculture suffered, yet Mohammad Shah Rangila (like Jahandar Shah before him and Zafar later) continued to celebrate the 'glories of Sawan' with great zest. No wonder the dancing girls of Chawri Bazar made good money, for the raindrops were akin to pearls being scattered by *mast* (heady) Sawan right up to the royal swings at Mehrauli that wafted princes and princesses into a veritable fairyland, till Bhadon's *badaria* (small mass of dark cloud) had deposited its naughty load of pent-up moisture on lovers' hideouts.

One was reminded of this as late as the 1960s when dancing girls were particularly active in the Walled City. They found many customers while Sawan showered its bounty. There were two prominent ones in Macchliwalan, both plump and attractive. Those were the days when the song, '*Sawan ka mahina/Pawan kare sor* (not shor)' was heard all over. Those two, who addressed each other as Lata (to hide their identity), would sing it with such verve that customers would just fall for their wiles.

One afternoon, after a sultry week, it began to rain heavily and the two 'Latas' (green bangles in chubby hands, *gunghroos* on their feet) danced with gusto in the courtyard of a hotel to cries of '*Sawan aiyo jhoom ke*', while their *dupattas* rippled in the balmy breeze. Now no 'Latas' presumably sing to welcome the romantic season, for the rains get scarcer every year because of the truancy of '*Sawan ke badlon*' (rain-clouds) in these increasingly mundane times. Blame it on El Nino if it helps.

May Queen at Ludlow Castle

As we enter the month of May, with roses blooming all over and May Queen contests being planned in hotels, restaurants, clubs and residential colonies, one's thoughts go back to the 1890s, which saw Delhi's first May Queen being selected. This is as per hearsay. Some however, claim that the first such event did not take place during the viceroyalty of Lord Curzon but when Lord Lytton as Governor General came here in 1877. Going by what Norah Nicholson used to say till her death as a nonagenarian many years ago, the first May Ball was held at Ludlow Castle, where the European Club had been moved from the Town Hall because of a plague epidemic scare in 1898. She had, as a young girl, heard from her grannies that the function saw the crowning of Miss Ball as May Queen. Could have been a memory lapse for the contest winner's father (Ball Sahib) was a noted magistrate at Agra in early 20th century and later migrated to South Africa where he set up a lucrative legal practice. His daughter (living in the house on the hill) became May Queen in the city of the Taj in the 1920s, long after the famous contest held at the Savoy in Mussoorie. According to the late Mrs Roberts, born in 1880, the name of the dimpled girl who won the title in Delhi was Heather Jones, and when she was crowned her admirers went wild with joy, while her rival Charmain Miller's supporters gulped down their disappointment with large pegs of whisky on a night which was unexpectedly cool for that part of the year because of a strong breese blowing from the Ridge.

Among those present were the Houghtons, Campbells, a visiting writer, Miss Saunders, Mr Maidens, who founded Maidens Hotel, a number of CMS clergymen and a Catholic priest of St. Mary's Church. This reverend Father impressed on the gathering that the first-ever May Queen was the Virgin Mary, to whom the month of May is devoted. Present also were the proprietors of London Stores, Spencer's and Carlton's from Kashmere Gate. Some Punjabi Muslim shoe merchants (who came to Delhi during the time of Shah Alam) and the Khatri businessmen, who settled down during the reign of Shahjahan, also managed to enter Ludlow Castle hall. It's worth mentioning that the Kaum Punjabian's main face at that time was the Hanafi Siddiqui, whose family was more interested in setting up printing presses, madarasas and building mosques. The Khatris were headed by Lala Chunna Mal who, along with other elite, both Muslim and Hindu, used to 'take the air' in the spacious Kashmere Gate area, then the lungs of the city. The most boisterous were the Tommies from the Red Fort and Daryaganj. They had come in their one-horse carriages, sounding trumpets, blowing whistles and raising hurrahs before parking their Ticca gharries at the hackney carriage stand on Ludlow Castle Road, which continued to exist till the early 1970s.

If one were to go by the treatise, *Delhi between Two Empires* that was the time when many of the Mirzas and Mirs had come down a step or two from their high pedestal to become school teachers and clerks because of income constraints. Better off than them were the *karkhanedars* or owners of small factories. One wonders how many of these neo-rich managed to be at the club which had presumably relaxed its rules for the much-touted May Queen show.

According to historian Naryani Gupta, the Civil Lines had ceased to be the main residential area for the Europeans by then and 'second-class Europeans' had begun to settle down north of Qudsia Garden and Nicholson Park. They were mostly Telegraph and Railway employees, like the ones depicted in the film 'Julie', in which Om Prakash plays the role of a bottle-happy Anglo-Indian dad.

To select the May Queen may not have been the railwaymen's prerogative but their presence at the renamed Delhi Club could not be overlooked as Heather's father was a senior railway engine driver, Charmain Miller, first runner-up 'and taller by far, burst into tears, burying her sweet face in her delicate hands as her boyfriend tried to comfort her with umpteen kisses', recalled Mrs Roberts in the 1960s. The May Queen contests now are more lavish and popular but somehow one always thinks that the cultural pastures were greener when the Civil Lines was the centre of fashion, with hotels like Lauries, Cecil, Suisse and Maidens vying with each other. Railwaymen did not usually frequent them but still they formed an influential community since New Year's Eve 1867, when the first train arrived in Delhi and its whistle was heard in the Walled City.

FAITH AND MYSTERY

The faith of our fathers
Holy faith
We will be true to thee
Till death
Hymn

Faith and Quaint Sensation

There's a mini-park in Mayfair Gardens bungalow locality, touching the walls of Siri fort, where is situated the 15th century tomb of Makhdum Sahib, visited by devotees throughout the year. Sheikh Makhdum Sabzwari came to Delhi from Sabzwar, in Central Asia, at the end of the reign of Bahlul Lodi (1451–1489) or the beginning of his son, Nizam Khan Sikandar Lodi's (1489–1517) reign, says Sadia Dehlvi in her book on Sufi shrines of Delhi.

One is not sure about the identity of this saint but it is said that he had been directed in a dream to go to India and preach there. Makhdum Sahib's Sufi discourses were ardently heard by those who visited his jungle abode, where wild animals roamed about but did not harm anyone because of the influence of the saint, says a legend. Eventually, the Lodi Sultan (father or son) heard of him and invited the dervish to the royal court. He went there reluctantly and came back dissatisfied with the sultan's conduct.

Perhaps, realising that he had offended the sheikh, the sultan while out hunting one day, decided to visit his *khanqah* or hospice. What he saw there amazed him, for Makhdum Sahib was feeding a wild leopard a bunch of grass as though it was a goat. The sultan immediately dismounted from his horse and after offering his salaam decided to sit in a corner. The leopard was ordered to leave by the saint who then turned his attention to the sultan. The latter apologised for having been rude at the court and requested him not to leave his kingdom but continue to reside in it and bless its subjects.

Makhdum Sahib nodded and gave the sultan (Bahlul or Sikandar) a *tawiz* or amulet which he had brought from Mecca. He told him so long it was tied to his arm or that of his successors, the sultanate would continue to flourish; otherwise it would be conquered by an invader who and his descendants would rule long, undisturbed. The sultan took the *tawiz*, salaamed the saint again, mounted his horse and rode away. As history shows, the third ruler of the dynasty, Ibrahim Lodi lost the kingdom in 1526 to Babar, with whom the Mughal dynasty started and continued to rule India until 1858, when Queen Victoria proclaimed herself empress and Bahadur Shah Zafar was exiled to Rangoon.

One tends to believe the story about the saint's prediction but at the same time wonders what happened to the amulet. Did Ibrahim Lodi forget to tie it at the fateful First Battle of Panipat or did the *tawiz* somehow get lost? May be yes or no; also the prediction may not have been wholly true after all. But standing in front of the mazar of Makhdum Sahib one tries to banish these thoughts lest they be regarded as sacrilegious.

The reason for visiting the mosque and mazar of Makhdum Sahib was a strange story related by Hafiz Manzoor Ahmed of Basti Nizamuddin during a winter evening in 1981. Hafiz died not long after, but what he said continued to feed one's curiosity for the past 33 years until the temptation to visit Makhdum Sahib's shrine could no longer be resisted. According to him, there was a widow named Nadira whose husband Saddique had died without leaving an heir. Nadira was 55 years old, lonely and sad when she came to the shrine one afternoon in the first decade of the 20th century. She had either been told by somebody or had the urge herself to pray there. And the prayer was strange, for a woman of her age. She sought the saint's blessing for a son who could continue his father's lineage. She prayed with tears in her eyes and all at once experienced a sensation which passed through her face, bosom and lower abdomen and then ceased to excite her. Nadira then had a great urge to go to the toilet, but as there was none near the shrine she squatted under a tree. When she got up she felt as though she had just conceived. The widow went home dazed and had a dream the same night in which she saw a bearded old man blessing her and confirming that her wish had been fulfilled.

Believe it or not, nine months later Nadira gave birth to a son who was strange in his behaviour at first and did not either speak or walk properly. But after three years he began to improve and by the time he was five was able to attend school. He turned out to be a brilliant student and following graduation secured a good government job. His name was Javed and after he got married and became the father of twin boys, Nadira died. Javed migrated to Karachi and what happened to him and his family was not known to Manzoor Ahmed. But one supposes it flourished with the saint's blessing.

Incidentally, Makhdum Sahib's tomb is still in a fairly good condition on Khel Gaon Marg, its stone-domed roof (with four decorative minars) supported on 12 pillars. Both the tomb and the mosque on the north are protected monuments. The masjid has several prayer chambers and a fluted roof. However, the huge gate near it, which was probably from the Tughlak times, is not in a good state of preservation though it too is protected by the ASI.

Omens and Visions of 1857

Whenever the anniversary of the 1857 Revolt comes around, one is reminded of the omens and weird events that preceded it. In Delhi the 'Angel of Death' was seen hovering over the Red Fort, an apparition also witnessed before the death of Aurangzeb in February 1707. A headless warrior riding a horse startled many a traveller near the Kashmere Gate. He came to be known as the *dund* or man with just a neck sticking out above his shoulders. The *dund* was also seen in Bareilly, Agra, Lucknow and Faizabad. And wherever he went there was bloodshed. In Agra, reported the *Statesman* before the onset of the summer of 1857, a sheet of blood was seen on several nights in the sky that seemed to extend right up to Delhi and beyond. The maulvi of Faizabad, Ahmedullah Shah, who later led the heroic resistance in Lucknow, is said to have dreamt that Delhi's streets were flowing with blood that had seeped into Payawan, the place where he was eventually killed.

Strange sightings were reported on the Ridge too, by English soldiers. One of them saw a long line of kings silently trooping down to the city and then disappearing. Another soldier saw his dead father wagging his finger as though warning him of lurking dangers. A British woman, Harriet Tytler, wife of Capt. Robert Tytler, dreamt that the baby she was carrying in her womb would have to pass through a harowing time until both she and her child were rescued by Punjabi or Pathan sepoys. Harriet did in fact give birth on the Delhi Ridge and her baby nearly died of dysentery during the rains that followed. However, she was able to take the child safely to Karnal.

In Shahjahanpur, the daughter of a Protestant priest had a nightmare in which she saw a whole lot of people being shot in the church, among them her father. She also saw a man in black walking in her house after midnight. The spectre would always disappear near the staircase. Her dream came true as on a May morning in 1857 rebel sepoys attacked the church and killed nearly all the male members, including the girl's father. But she and her mother escaped, only to be taken captive by a Pathan who kept pressurising her to marry him. That she narrowly managed to avert a forced wedding and returned home with her mother, after saving the Pathan and his family from the raiding Firangi troops is another story.

In Chandni Chowk a Sikh *sevadar* saw a vision of men hanging from gibbets that extended from Lal Mandir to Fatehpuri Mosque. Later, it turned out that the avenging British did hang many sepoys and others they suspected of taking part in the revolt from gibbets in the Chowk.

The grandmother of Haji Zahur was troubled by dreams in which she saw dead bodies rotting in front of Gurdwara Sis Ganj, with an overwhelming stench that seemed to persist even after she woke up. As it turned out, the bodies of two sons and a grandson of Bahadur Shah Zafar, who had been killed by Lt Hodson at the Khooni Darwaza, were thrown to rot in front of the gurdwara at the spot now marked by Northbrook Fountain.

Lala Hanwant Sahai, who was arrested in the Hardinge Bomb Case of 1912, told this scribe in the 1960s that his father's elder sister used to see an Angrez family being massacred in the building of the Delhi Bank, just across her house. The dream recurred for three nights and on the last night she imagined she could even hear the screams of a woman and her daughters. The dream came true when the manager of the bank, Beresford, his wife and daughters met their end at the hands of the rebels on May 11. They put up a brave resistance, with Mrs Beresford killing two of the attackers before being done to death herself.

In Daryaganj, the *nehar* that flowed through it was reportedly seen to be covered with blood by a relative of Sir Sayyid Ahmad Khan—or this is what his dream foretold. When Sir Sayyid, then 40 years old, came to inspect his house after the disturbances were quelled, he found it in bad shape, but whether the relative escaped is not known. At the Khooni Darwaza or Lal Darwaza of Allauddin, a man walking towards the Delhi Gate one evening saw blood trickling down as though somebody had been murdered there. And at a shrine near the Jamuna a naked faqir was heard chanting, '*Mar, mar*' at the beginning of May 1857. Another faqir in Shahjahanpur made his *takia* (abode) ring with the same chant, as recorded by J.F. Fanthome in his novel *Mariam*, which also gave a graphic description of the church massacre.

What does one make of these uncanny happenings? Do coming events cast their shadow, especially of macabre incidents? One doesn't know but then all the witnesses could not be lying. Incidentally, modern research has proved that the mind has infinite capacities of foresight. May be what are termed as gloomy pre-'Mutiny' yarns were not just balderdash.

Weird and Uncanny

There was a pretty girl in the flats opposite Hari Nagar in Delhi who used to give flying kisses to the seething sun every evening and mutter. 'Darling, darling bad behman'—dishonest beloved. Sometimes she would add a naughty expletive that shocked the passers-by. Rickshaw pullers and street urchins would watch, but from a distance, and women out shopping for milk and vegetables would shake their heads in astonishment.

Sometimes her mother would ventures out from the flat in which they lived and gesture to the girl to come home. But she would still linger on, unmindful of the stares directed at her deeply engrossed in her daily ritual. One often wondered what had affected her so much. Was it a love affair that had failed?

There was another young woman, always dressed in a blouse and petticoat, with a garland round her neck, a red tilak on the forehead and a paan in her mouth, who used to keep winking while walking on the road to Subhash Nagar.

Also, in a West Delhi colony was a girl who would come out in mid-afternoon, when the sun was at its scorching worst and walk briskly up and down 'E Street', opposite Metal Forgings. She was slim and sallow-complexioned, wearing salwar-kameez and leather slippers, which probably aided her to make at least a hundred rounds of the street. If someone looked at her, she would stop and stare back before resuming her marathon walk. Some said both the woman in a petticoat and victims of trauma.

An old man with tousled hair and grisly chin, in a crumpled-up shirt and pyjamas who sneezed and clapped by turns, came to the area in the morning, before most people were up, picking up bits of cigarette paper and odds and ends that attracted his attention. He was neither mad, nor a rag-picker, but the grandfather of a lower-strata family living in the Government Press Quarters, would occasionally be seen buying milk from the DMS depot. The funny old man too has disappeared somewhere.

An old woman who lived near the Kucha Tihar Mosque was usually spotted standing near its boundary wall, softly repeating. 'Khizr, Khizr'. While enquiries about the other odd characters failed to elicity any plausible explanation, the whispers of the old woman did. A venerable maulana, with long hair and graceful beard, confided that was Hajjan. But was referring to Khwaja and thereby hangs a tale.

'Khwaja Khizr', the name brings to mind an evening in the University campus, when the walk from St. Stephen's College seemed a particularly long one for two young men, new to Delhi. 'It might take more than half and hour to make it to Kashmere Gate bus stand, and it's dark already; may Khwaja Khizr help us', said Baig as he looked at the winding road thrown into darkness by a long blackout during the Indo-Park war. 'Who is Khwaja Khizr?' Was the natural question from the perplexed scribe still learning the ropes in Ink Street.

Baig looked to his left and right and replied: 'He's the one who takes care of the wayfarers. When in danger, one must invoke him, Khizr, which means green. It is believed, by some, to have accompanied Prophet Abraham to Canaan, by others, the person who guided Moses and the Israelits during their 40-year journal to the Promised Land. Yet others, believe that he was the great grandson of Shem, the son of Noah, and one of the survivors of the Deluge. The Greek belief is that he accompanied Alexander on his conquests as friend, philosopher and guide. He was also the saint who controlled the waters of immortality.

Belief in Khwaja Khzir can be traced to almost all religions, including Judaism, Christainity and Islam. For the Sindhis he is Jhule Lal or Raja Khidar and in Punjab he is supposed to be an avtar of Vishnu, says William Dairymple. When one is in danger, one has to call to him thrice and he is there to help, never failing to respond in any emergency. The old woman of Tihar called on just by force of habit only twice and hence probably, got no response.

Perhaps, in the western milieu he came to be known as St. Christopher. This saint is revered in the East too, for even in Delhi one sees many car owners who have a medal of St. Christopher dangling from the steering wheel. Whether there is substance in the belief or not is a moot point, but it is a good psychological boost alright.

Mystic Haunts at the Kotla

When Firoz Shah Tughlak built his *kotla* or fort in the 14th century, he did not have to look far for a site. The ruins of an earlier citadel were already there and these belonged to the time of the slave sultans. Some aver that they were actually part of the ancient Indraprastha. Such conjectures are natural in a city like Delhi where there are several layers of habitation, for isn't the city older than Rome and even the Ilium of the Trojans, from where Aeneas escaped to establish another city state after the tragic affair with Queen Dido? For that matter even the Red Fort occupies the site of an old Afghan fort. And to go back further, the fortifications of Alauddin Khilji extended right up to the place where now stands the Khooni Darwaza.

Firoz Shah's Kotla was an excellent specimen of Tughlak architecture, for he was a builder of magnificent monuments, like Shahjahan in a later age. But when the Sayyids came to power in 1414 they shifted their attention to another part of the city which included Mubarakpur, the present Ramakrishna Puram and Lodhi Gardens area. The Lodis, of course, did not lay the gardens now known after them. Though there is a profusion of Lodi monuments there, these gardens were laid in their present form in the early 1930s and known after Lady Willingdon, the Vicereine. When the Mughals took over, Kotla was a forsaken building and the haunt of Sufis and Mast Qalandars. The latter were a sect of dervishes who wore camel-skin shirts or just wrapped themselves up in blankets. They were generally big, sturdy men, neglectful of their hygiene, who went about beating themselves with iron chains or brandishing huge steel *chimtas* or fire-tongs. Ahmad Ali, the author of *Twilight in Delhi*, talks of a Mast Qalandar who hadn't brushed his teeth for years, with the result that pieces of meat kept sticking to them and emitted a bad odour. He, like the rest of his tribe, came to the Jama Masjid area from the Kotla, especially during the time of the various urs.

Now you do not find Mast Qalandars in the Kotla, but the Sufis are still there. Go on a Thursday and you will find them in full sway. People do not flock to see them but seek the intervention of jinns in their daily lives. The jinns have been associated with the Kotla ever since it became a discarded citadel. It is believed that they were formed from fire and not earth, like man, during the time of creation. There are two kinds of jinns, the *tairan* and the *haiwan*. While the former are blessed beings that help mankind and even takes wives from it, the latter are destructive and hostile in their dealings because of their baser instincts. William Dalrymple mentions *dijjns* in his famous book on Delhi. They are also found in Mehrauli around the Makan-e-Khizr.

Hazrat Khizr is believed to be the grandson of Adam, the first man who keeps travelling around the world. His journey will terminate only when the world ends. By the way, jinns are fond of sweets and pretty women. They are dressed in white and being invisible, cast no shadows.

Interestingly, people of all faiths throng the Kotla to seek the blessings of the jinns. So there is a regular mela there on Thursdays. Some will remember that many years ago the King of the jinns was supposed to get married on a certain day somewhere in Iran. Reports in newspaper quoted mystics to be urging people to seek boons during the mythical event, with a stern warning to those who tried to scoff at the idea. The reverberations were felt in the Kotla too, where jinns were seen frolicking at night after consuming milk in mud *kulhars*. Several of these were recovered the next day and many wondered how they got there.

One remembers the tale of the midwife who was blindfolded and led away one night to a dilapidated house in Delhi. When she opened her eye she saw a woman in labour and after the delivery was escorted back safe and sound with a present of a handful of coals, which turned into gold coins when she reached home and threw them down in disgust. But do not expect the ones at the Kotla to repeat the act.

Strange Practices and Beliefs

T.S. Eliot wrote, 'I will show you fear in a handful of dust.' This is what one finds in confirmation at the Yamuna ghat where *aghories* and tantrics are found, supposedly raising devils from the river sand at midnight.

A man named Kapoor went to a tantric seeking help from his arch rival, Gupta (both names changed). He had learnt that the opponent was preparing to release a blood *handi* (vessel full of blood) which would go flying to cause his death. The tantric asked Kapoor to find another tantric who could ward off the fatal *handi* by reciting the appropriate mantra to reverse its direction.

The other long-held belief is that if a person sees such a *handi* (in which is a wooden liver and heart submerged in blood that keeps rotating while the *handi* is in motion) he should sit up and tell the occult vessel to return to the one who sent it. Then the charm is reversed and the rival has little chance of escape. This piece of research has been done by Vijay N. Shankar. Shankar has spent close to five years on such subjects and the result is his treatise, *Shadow Boxing with the Gods*.

Another reference by him is to the jinns of Firoz Shah Kotla. When a businessman fell asleep in the Kotla gardens, a jinn who lived nearby appeared to him in a dream and asked the man to get a sackful of charcoal as an offering. The businessman did so and on the next day, a Thursday (sacred to jinns), felt so tired that he fell asleep. Late in the evening when he got up, he found that the charcoal had turned into gold coins.

Then there was a homeopath of Gali Bathashan in the Walled City who practiced in a clinic full of dust some years ago. A patient who asked him why he did not clean the place was told that a jinn had appeared to him when he used to work as a tailor and told him to cure people instead, with a special powder he recommended, and also never to clear the dust in which the jinn said he had taken up abode. The patient was given three small sachets of the powder and assured that he would be cured without the need of a second visit. Hard to believe but not for the one who underwent the cure.

A Tamilian astrologer, Shankar, I chanced to meet, had with him palm leaves on which were inscribed in an ancient Tamil script prophecies regarding any individual who happened to seek urgent help. Called *nadi* leaf it is believed to have been written upon by Agastya (the Puranic rishi who crossed the Vindhya Range into South India never to return again to the North). Thousands of such leaves are stored in neatly stringed bundles to facilitate sifting by astrologer families in and around the Vaitheeswaram temple of Chennai. Besides fortune telling the nadi readers also suggest curative measures to overcome problems of karma. The Ganda nadi talks of a person's past, present and future and is mostly concerned with material needs.

A contrast to them are the Haridwar registers. The *pandas* or pandits there show pilgrims who seek their help, signed messages written by their forefathers during earlier visits. How they do it is a closely guarded secret of the *pandas* who have been living on the

Ganga banks for hundreds of years. However, modern-day *pandas*, who have taken to computers and smartphones, are sometimes willing to talk about the mystery. There are thousands of red cloth- bound registers called Lal Kitab marked with symbols, noting town, family surname and address. When a visitor mentions the name of his forebear and town of origin, the *panda* is able to find the relevant red book and satisfy his curiosity. This indigenous and ingenious system has worked for centuries.

There is no fear of terror involved here unless one antagonises the *pandas*. But not so in a Kali temple, where earlier human and now animal sacrifice are made. A holy man, much respected by the author, had this to say: 'These things crept into religious practices because of powerful priests who have always used fear to over-awe followers'. Eliot had been much influenced by Eastern thought and precepts, ending his famous work, *The Wasteland* with the words, 'Ahom Shanti, Shanti'. And that's what probably banishes fear as perceived by the poet.

The Coming of Lisbeth Jane

Sometimes a man's death opens up a flood of memories. Father Ian Charles Weatherall who passed away last month aged 91 had served in the 16th Punjab Regiment during World War II. A Scotsman, he decided to make Delhi his home in 1951 after joining the Cambridge Brotherhood. Among his friends, while he was pastor of St. James's Church in Kashmere Gate, was Alfred J. Edwin, one of the well-known writers in the capital in those days. Once Edwin wrote a story about an Anglo-Indian family of Nicholson Road and showed it to Father Weatherall. After reading it the Anglican priest shook his head and asked Edwin if he intended getting the story published. 'Who would believe it?' replied Edwin and left it on his table.

Allen Alexander, great-grandson of a legendary Major of the 1919 Afghan War, who lived with Weatherall as a guest for some time, picked it up because of his love for ghost stories and was allowed to keep the manuscript. The young man shared a flat in Daryaganj with this scribe in 1970–71 and gave the story to him to read.

Allen, unfortunately, died in Faridabad 18 years ago, predeceasing his father Harvey, World War veteran and later pilot of the private plane of the Maharaja of Cooch Behar, whose daughter Gyatri Devi became Maharani of Jaipur. If memory serves right, this is the gist of what Alfred J. Edwin wrote, based on an account by a deceased girl's tantric uncle who claimed to have witnessed her nocturnal visits:

When Lisbeth Jane died in 1928, (the same year as her favourite novelist, Thomas Hardy), her parents were greatly grieved. She was their only daughter and just 20 years old. The end came suddenly after an epileptic fit. Tall, slim, fair and pretty, she had been a brilliant student, fond of reading and writing. She liked English classics and wrote love poetry without being emotionally attached to anyone, except the penniless Francis Thompson of *The Hound of Heaven* fame (incidentally this metaphysical poem was read out by Rajaji to Mahatma Gandhi while the two were in British jail together). As the only issue, she was naturally the apple of her parents' eyes, who doted over their daughter. Her passing away was a big shock not only to them but also to other relatives, friends and acquaintances. There was one boy who fancied himself to be in love with her. He was so overcome with grief that he left Delhi soon after to join the Royal Navy but was killed during the Japanese attack on the Andamans.

There were pictures of Jane in various poses hanging in the 19th century house which were an ever-present reminder and a solace to her father and mother. It seemed she lived in between those golden frames and had never parted from them. Sometimes they wondered how the grave could hold such a vibrant young soul. It seems they were right or this is what a tantric told them: At 2.30 am she would begin stirring in her grave.

The tombstone vibrated and slowly lifted up. It took Jane five minutes to get out and 10 minutes to reach home. Sometimes a belated passerby saw a beautiful girl moving fast on Lothian Road as though on skates. The door was closed, but she wafted into her room, preserved as in her lifetime. She gazed at her pictures, her books, the furniture, and the gramophone. Then one by one she visited all the rooms in the house, including the one in which her parents were sound asleep. Then she moved to the balcony from which she used to call the 'chiz-wallahs', the sellers of *chaat, kulfi, jalebis, kacchoris, gajak*, popcorn and the seasonal fruits. She loved phalse, which came in May and lasted just a month, followed by jamuns and mangoes, which got bigger and juicer as the monsoon advanced and the koel's call increased in intensity.

Jane would stand in the balcony during her nocturnal visits. Then she would move to the terrace and the verandah. She had been in the house for an hour and now it was time to make the return journey. But before leaving she had one last peep into her parents' bedroom. They slept soundly. She blew a kiss to them and wafted out of the main door.

Jane would look sad but she had only limited time at her disposal. She would walk swiftly back to Lothian cemetery and reach there in 10 minutes flat. The tombstone would open automatically and in five minutes she was inside. The last thing she probably heard was the cock crowing in the distance to announce the return of morning and then her long sleep till the next night began.'

During his stay at Jane's house, the tantric uncle felt strange vibrations one night, got up and saw Jane entering and leaving the house. After that he saw her every night during his prolonged stay and even heard her talking to herself. But her parents never could see her except in dreams.

Once the tantric uncle followed Jane to the cemetery on a bicycle and saw the weird happenings there, even as matutinal sephyr frolicked in her tresses. Sikandar, the night chowkidar, corroborated what the tantric said. He had witnessed an ethereal form hovering over a tombstone and vanishing, only to be back before early dawn and then finally disappearing into the marble grave, the roses on which were kept fresh by the dew falling down from the yellow laburnum tree.

One could not trace Jane's grave in the Lothian Road cemetery as most of the tombs in it are now without gravestones. Fr Weatherall did not know where it was and Alfred J. Edwin is long dead, but one of his strangest stories needs to be retold all the same, *mutatis mutandis*.

Delhi's Very Own Mysteries

Long before TV started its own horror series *Ahaat* and *Koi Hai*, it was stories related by word of mouth that kept the children of Delhi engrossed at bedtime. A favourite tale was that of the headless horseman, which has been told and retold for so many years that it has acquired may versions. Even now in some walled city homes you can hear it being related to children without access to TV.

There are other tales too about the supernatural whose horror potential is increased by the atmosphere that night imparts, not only in the landscape but also to living rooms in dingy houses, whose staircases begin to creak with nocturnal sounds and echoes that permeate lonely corners and make them look spooky. In Jama Masjid Gali Auila, dwells an octogenarian, Bibi Amma, along with her son and his family. Whenever the lights go off in the evening, the children activate a hurricane lantern and huddle close to the old woman. The power failure robs the street of its brightness and there is nothing one can do except stare in the dark and hear Bibi Amma's tale.

Playing on the terrace or in the balcony is out of the question and dinner is a long-delayed prospect. So the best thing is to hear stories and invest the darkness with the dazzling shapes of princes and princesses who live in times more exciting than the present, when TV is the only mode of recreation after sundown.

Bibi Amma is a paan addict. She eats several from morning to night to get over the boredom that afflicts people of her age. A *paan-dan* given to her in dowry is kept at her bedside and so she is able to help herself to the folded betel leaves whenever she feels like it. To chew away her disappointments has become a habit that keeps her in tune with the ties, though she mostly dwells in the past and sees the supposedly modern locality where she stays as an extension of her old *mohalla* in Shahjahanpur.

The children become impatient and the story begins. It dates back to the 19th century, when a Seth returning home one night came across a weird man riding a horse. It was winter and the horseman had covered himself with a cloak. The Seth got scared but the stranger hailed him as if to allay his fears and gave him a bag which was very light.

They soon parted company and when the Seth reached his house he opened the bag and found three gold *mohurs* in it. Believe it or not, they were the ones he had lost while gambling on Diwali night. That was not a big loss, but it set a chain reaction and the merchant had gradually lost all his wealth. The night he was accosted by the strange rider meant a swing in fortune and he did not regret the meeting.

'Who was the strange horseman,' asks Bibi Amma. A 'ghost, a ghost,' cry the elder children in a chorus. 'No,' says the old woman. 'It is the nocturnal horseman, and wherever he goes he scatters wealth. He was in Shahjahanpur 150 years ago when the *kali andhi* tornado struck. Next, he was seen in Rampur and Bareilly, and the year I was engaged he was sighed in Agra. It is Delhi's turn next, for he moves about in a cycle of decades. He was also sighed before the Mutiny of 1857, but then his appearance forebode evil happenings.'

Just then the lights came on, but the children have been looking for the strange horseman ever since. Their grandmother cannot be wrong. This conviction has invested their humdrum street with a mystery where every alley seems to beckon the midnight rider who scatters wealth. There is something which TV can never do, for how can it compete with Bibi Amma?

There is another well-known tale about a midwife who delivered a jinn's child and got more than a handful of gold coins for her labours.

She and her daughter concluded that it was a gift from the jinns known to help human beings. Incidentally, some places in the Red Fort were believed to be haunted by jinns. Just before Partition, an English soldier on guard duty is reported to have fainted after seeing a pair of female hands circling round his head. His commanding officer thought that he must have been drunk, but a similar sight was witnessed by Asghar Ali Khan. Custodian of the fort in the 1960s. A photographer of a national daily even spent a night in the Diwan-e-Am but only saw some shadows. Not long after Asghar Ali Khan retired and the Army authorities came out with a contradiction, but Bibi Amma is not aware of this and the ex-custodian's claim become part of her tale of the strange horseman.

Nostalgic Medley

Gently walk, O fairest one
Lest your comely waist be sprained
Urdu Couplet

Delhi of Ahmed Ali

'Although the friends are oblivious of my being, I have a thousand associations with them'. The lines are from Hafiz as quoted by Professor Ahmed Ali, who died at Karachi some years ago. And in a way what Hafiz said was true of Ahmed Ali too, for though he had left Delhi after Partition his heart was very much in the Walled City where he was born and grew up in a haveli.

Elder son of Syed Shujauddin, Assistant Commissioner in Punjab, he did not become a doctor in accordance with his father's wishes but cultivated a taste for literature, both Urdu and English. As a matter of fact, 'he read English fiction camouflaged by the covers of a maths book', or stories in Urdu which were considered obscene by his family. Taking his degree in English Literature from Lucknow University, he became a professor and later a diplomat.

However, Ahmed Ali will not be remembered as a teacher or diplomat but as the author of two famous books, *Twilight in Delhi* and *Ocean of Night*—at least for the English reading public though his output in Urdu was greater, reflecting leftist views influenced as he was by such progressives as Sahibzada Mahmooduzzafar Khan, Sajjad Zaheer and Dr Rashid Jehan.

One can visualise the Aldous Huxley look-alike professor in a three-piece suit, with a bow and matching handkerchief, who walked with hasty steps through the *galis* and *kuchas* of Delhi. His usual walk included a round of Chandni Chowk, Ballimaran, Chawri Bazaar, Jama Masjid, Matia Mahal—as far as Haveli Sadar Sadur where once Ghalib used to sit and recite in the evening in twilight in Delhi his character Mir Ashiq—after whom a *kucha* in Chawri Bazaar is named—used to take such a walk every night.

Twilight in Delhi, which actually lamented the fall of the Mughals and the advent of the British, is a work which will never grow old so long as the walled city exists. The *sabeel* or water-hut which Ahmed Ali described with such zest is still there at the entrance of Ballimaran. The travails of the family of Mir Nihal are even now those of most middle-class Muslims whose lives revolve around the Jama Masjid. The pigeon fanciers, the Mast Qalandars, Kambal Shahs wrapped in patchy blankets, the milk sellers, the *kababias* and the eunchs—they are all there but with different names. Only the likes of Babban Jaan and Mushtari Bai have moved out of Chawri Bazaar and now hold their *mujras* in the dirty kothas of G.B. Road.

Mehrauli too continues as old, with its monuments just as they were at the time of Mir Nihal, so also Basti Nizamuddin. Chowk in Lucknow has lost its glamour but many of the decadent nawabs like Chhakkan still inhabit their havelis though the world outside has changed a lot and it's difficult to find a coy Huma Jaan.

Ahmed Ali did not return to Delhi after his migration to Pakistan. Once, not so long ago, as a transit passenger he stayed put in the plane, declining to see the city he loved so much because he feared it might have changed beyond recognition.

Be that as it may, one of his last actions relating to the city of his birth was a meeting at Karachi with William Dalrymple, author of the *City of Jinns*, who had gone to seek his advice on the old culture of Shahjehanabad, particularly the Sufi tradition.

When the 'ocean of night' encompasses Delhi and Lucknow and someone recites '*Phoolon ka rang kuch angur ka arq/Koi haram cheez nahin hai shaab mein'*, one is reminded of the redolent evenings of Ahmed Ali's times when the juice of the grape ceased to be the forbidden drink. One emerges then into the lanes to hear the old vagabond sing, 'May Lucknow last beyond all harm, it still is better than many a place, for you can often here behold, a lovely and enticing face.'

Such sounds and sights had however, long ceased to exist for Ahmed Ali at the beautiful house in Hyder Ali Road Karachi, in which he and his wife, the Urdu writer, Bilqees Jahan dwelt with their three sons and daughter after 'twilight in Delhi'. But he did think often of Munshi Prem Chand and Shahid Suhrawardy—and of *Hamari Gali*, the like of which Karachi did not possess.

The Heritage of ICS Men

It was Ruskin Bond who got one interested in the writings of Indian Civil Service men through the book he edited on ghost stories of the Raj days. Some of the officers had served in Delhi and taken the trouble of producing the Delhi Gazetteer of 1883-1884 while another one, H.R. Nevill, went on to complete the Agra District Gazetteer in 1900. Among these men were such luminaries as C.A. Kincaid, whose *The Tale of the Tulsi Plant and Other Stories* is still popular.

J.S. Lall, who came to Delhi as a secretary in the Central Govt after being commissioner of the vast Agra Division, belonged to a distinguished family of the Walled City whose ancestor Chandu Lal migrated to Lahore after the Revolt of 1857. He claimed descent from Raja Todar Mal, Akbar's revenue minister. A great friend of Khushwant Singh's, Lall never mentioned his full name—John Stanley Lall—till he retired and started writing books.

Lall's book *Begum Samru: Fading Portrait in a Gilded Frame* which is the well-researched account of the Begum whom Shah Alam was supposed to have endeared as his own daughter after she saved Delhi from an invasion by the Sikhs under Baghel Singh. John Lall's brother, Arthur Lall, who became Permanent Representative of India to the United States, wrote his well-known book *The House at Adampur* on the family history.

J.M. Lobo Prabhu was a 'pucca sahib' like R.K. Nehru and B.K. Nehru, and his wife (40-odd years younger), Louella Lobo Prabhu was an attraction whenever she came to Delhi. The couple stayed after retirement at their Chateau de Lou in Mangalore. The suave E. N. Mangatrai also drew a crowd of admires whenever he visited the capital. His personality was such that one felt instinctively drawn to the man. It was said of him, like R.L.S., that the style was the man. Pran Nevile, 92, ex-diplomat, remembers him from Lahore days and his close relationship with Vijaylakshmi Pandit's daughter Nayantara with whom he later settled down. B.D. Sanwal wrote the well-illustrated *Agra and its Monuments* in the 1960s. He was Commissioner after Lall and an ardent student of history.

Going into earlier times, A.C. Renny, District Magistrate, found the time to write and study life in India and to come out with a story like *The Fire Jogi*. The Jogi (sic) not only commanded tigers and elephants but also predicted the future, like the death of his friend. Renny was in the same class of writers as the non-ICS Lafcadio Hearn, John Lang, who defended the Rani of Jhansi at the Calcutta and London courts, Hilton Brown, F. R. Corson and F. W. Bain, whose stories were edited by Ruskin Bond in a book of ghost stories.

But one sahib went one better by weaving a tale of the Roshanara Bagh with its weird midnight bearded, treetop hookah smoker. Sir Tej Bahadur Sapru said in 1946 that he had come across several European members of the Indian Civil Services who wrote graceful Persian and Urdu verse and also spoke with great facility. About Thomas Conlan, who once appeared in a case of divorce and dower, Sapru says: 'I have never heard in my life in court a better Urdu speech and one could hardly believe that the speaker was a genuine Irishman and not a man from Lucknow or Delhi...and as he warmed up, he quoted Ghalib and Momin on several occasions...'

H. J. Evans, Deputy Commissioner of Delhi just before Partition, too delivered a high-class speech at a *mushaira* and some could not believe their ears that an Englishman could speak such eloquent Urdu. The heritage of these ICS men is one that will never fade. Surprisingly few IAS officials do such creative writing now.

Mystic Thought and Poetry

Mysticism—the very world is swathed in mystery, and as such attracts by the infinite possibilities that it unfolds. Even the night watchman has a bit of mystery clinging to him. There is that wonderful quotation from the Bible.

> Watchman what of the night
> Watchman what of the night
> The watchman says
> Morning comes and also the night.

One senses the philosophy behind it, which is based on the acceptance of the present with fortitude in the hope of a bright future. Not only that, it shows the linking of two extremes, night and morning and its mystic union and, one daresay, of other parts of the day like the afternoon scenario of electric bulbs, dreaming in vacancy of the evening.

When mysticism comes into poetry, it imparts to it an additional attraction. The charm of John Donne's poetry lies in its mystic thought, and those who followed him right down to our own century have had their share of the cake.

That trend of thought is not confined to English literature alone. Patanjali recommended seven stages of sanctification to be experienced by the follower of the divine path of mysticism, recounts Rajendra Sarup Bhatnagar in his book, *Mysticism in Urdu Poetry*. The same path was divided by Buddha into four stages, which had to be crossed by the seeker of the Absolute.

The author works his way down to Muslim mysticism or Sufism. Those who choose this path, *tasawwuf*, follow the principle, 'lay aside what thou hast in thy head, to give way to what thou hast in thy hand, and not to retreat from whatever befalls thee' in the road to *tawhid* (god realisation). Abu Ali al-Rudhari points out, '*Tasawwuf* is to alight and abide at the Beloved's door, even though one is driven therefrom.' The beloved here, of course, is the Almighty. He who seeks this sort of knowledge needs the guidance of a pir or *shaikh*.

It is interesting to note that many of the early mystic poets of Urdu were dervishes. Dr Bhatnagar of the Department of

Philosophy, Allahabad University, mentions the interaction of Muslim holy men with Indian yogis as early as the 8th century in South India. They both influenced each other.

In the north, Sheikh Fariduddin Ganj Shakar (1173–1266), who lived in the 12th century, was a disciple of Khwaja Qutubuddin Bakhtiar Kaki of Mehrauli, and a follower of the Chishti *silsila* started by Khwaja Moinuddin. Sheikh Farid who laid the foundation for the incorporation of mystic thought into Urdu poetry, observes.

Waqt i sahr waqt i munjat hai
Khez daran waqt ki barkat hai
(The time of dawn is the real time for supplication
Awake because this is the time for the award of divine grace)

Sayyid Mohammad Husaini Gisudaraz Shahbaz, who died in 1421, was a disciple of Khwaja Nasiruddin Chiragh Delhi, the spiritual successor of Hazrat Nizammudin Auliya. Shahbaz is regarded as a learned Sufi poet. Then there were Shah Miranji of Bijapur, his disciple, Shah Janam, Sheikh Baha of Burhanpur, Shah Gamdhani of Gujarat, Mohammad Quli Qutab Shah of the Deccan who interpreted and developed Sufi doctrines in Diwani-I Urdu, having been influenced by Hafiz Shirazi. To him, 'love is the real cause of the origin and existence of everything'. These poets flourished from the 15th to the 17th centuries.

After Bahri, Shah Ahmed, Siraj, the great Shah Mir and Mazhar Jan Janan, who renounced the world for *shauq* or the passionate love of God, came Wali Dakhni, the father of Urdu poetry as we now know it. He made his mark in Sufism with the famous exclamation, 'O beloved, no thought of anything except of Thee enters into my heart'. His argument was that god could not be realised by those who used reason to search for him. That was the contention of Zahuruddin Hatim too.

Mir Taqi Mir, who lifted up the veils of the ghazal, was a mystic of note and followed the path shown by Ghazali and Ibn al-Arabhi. To him Dr Bhatnagar gives the credit for casting 'a far-reaching influence on the development of Sufi poetry'. Khwaja Mir Dard of the Nakshbandi sect is another great name.

Then comes Ghalib, great lover, greater mystic and the doyen of Urdu poetry, who ranks with Shakespeare himself. Mention must also be made of Niyaz Ahmed of Bareilly, Haidar Ali Atish, Alim Asi, Asghar, Aziz Raz and Bisheshwar Prasad Munawwar of Lucknow who died in 1970. The book ends with Munawwar's contribution to Indo-Muslim mystic thought. One must thank the Department of Islamic Studies, Jamia Hamdard, for his insight into a hitherto unknown realm to English readers.

It opens up the horizon to the winds that blew in from other climes and may well make the solitary night watchman echo the words of Arthur Hugh Clough:

> And not by eastern windows only
> When daylight comes, comes in the light
> In front the sun climbs slow, how slowly!
> But westward, look the land is bright!

The 'Ada' of Umrao Jaan

Those of us who have seen the film *Umrao Jaan* and those who have read the novel of the name, minus the second 'a' in 'Jaan' by Mirza Mahammad Hadi Ruswa, translated into English by Khushwant Singh and M.A. Husaini, will no doubt savour the beauty of the 19th century courtesan, not necessarily reflected in the countenance of the flamboyant Rekha.

It was so with friends who sat down on the terrace of a flat to celebrate the outbreak of the Mutiny in Delhi, which was a day after the events in Meerut on May 10.

One of them had come armed with a copy of *The Pursuit of Urdu Literature—A Select History* by Ralph Russell, an Englishman who had fallen in love with Urdu during the war years, published by Oxford University Press. The friend who had met Russell was reminded of other *sahibs* who had become equally enamoured of Urdu, George Puech who wrote under the pseudonym of 'Shor', foremost among them and Jamiat (Janet) Jan—the Major's wife, the most mysterious of them all. And both of them were contemporaries of Umrao, though the British lawyer whom Sir Tej Bahadur Sapru encountered in his younger days in a *munsif's* court in Allahabad belonged to a later age. The remarkable thing about the lawyer was that while arguing a case of dower and divorce, he spoke in Urdu, and as he warmed up he quoted Ghalib and Momin on several occasions to prove his point.

For those not familiar with the story, whenever a friend of Ruswa's came to Lucknow from Delhi he rented a small house to spend the evening with his companions. A thin partition separated this room from the neighbouring house in which dwelt an old courtesan. On such occasions an impromptu *mushaira* was usually held. At one such *mushaira* Ruswa's recital was followed by 'an exclamation of approval coming from the other side of the partition wall'. Later a maid of the courtesan came into the room and told Ruswa that her mistress wanted to meet him. That was how 'the first true novel in Urdu' got written and it turned out to be the life-story of Umrao Jan Ada—the courtesan who could recognise Ruswa by his voice, never having met him before that fateful evening.

By the terrace light someone read the couplet quoted by Marion Molteno, in her introduction to the book,

> *Khuda jab husn deta hai/Nazakat aa hi jaati hai*
> (When God bestows beauty, delicacy follows of its own accord)

to show 'the connection people (of the subcontinent) feel between poetry and the practicalities of everyday life'. She quoted another example from a friend who had not seen her for some time

> *Tumhari yaad jab aayee, tumhe jab dekhana chaha*
> *Falaq ke mah tare dekh kar hasrat mita Dali*
> (When I remembered you, when I longed to see you/I gazed at the heavens, at the moon and the stars and so banished my yearning)

Quite baffling to an English man or woman, who wouldn't quote Wordsworth, Shelley and Keats in like manner, but quite well understood in the common-day speech in our own climes.

The couplets that evening were dedicated to the unknown beauties of the Mutiny, both Indian and English, who had perished by the sword. Among them the friends of Mariam of Shahjahanpur, the fugititive

English woman made famous by J.F. Fanthome and Ruskin Bond, the daughters of the British banker, Baresford, of Chandni Chowk, the *begums* of Kashmere Gate, and the *khanums* of Barsha Mulla.

Long after these murders, special church services used to be held in Shahjahanpur, Meerut and Delhi for the victims of 1857 but gradually these were discontinued. But there are still people who remember such events though it's at a sundowner when poetry and anecdotes bring back the past to life and ada(grace) of Umrao Jan becomes a tantalising thought on a stuffy May day.

Noor Inayat Khan's Delhi Link

During the time of World War anniversaries few are aware that Noor Inayat Khan, super secret agent, had a close link with a Delhi shrine. And thereby hangs a tale that goes back to Tipu Sultan, who died fighting the British at Seringapatam during the Fourth Mysore War in 1799. Long after that one of his descendants founded a Sufi order in Delhi. Hazrat Inayat Khan, great-grandson of Tipu was a man of many tastes who went abroad in 1920 to give music concerts, having become a musician of note early in life.

He was initiated into Sufism by Sheikh Abu Hashim Madani but during a visit to the West wed an American woman, Ora Ray Baker (renamed Ameena) who gave birth to four children. According to Sadia Delhvi, Inayat Khan died in 1927 and was buried in Delhi, though he had settled down with his wife in Suresness, a Parisian suburb. His son, Pir Vilayat Khan succeeded him, whose successor was Pir Zia Khan, head of the Sufi Order International.

Inayat Khan's daughter, Noor Inayat Khan (just as famous as Mata Hari) was a British Special Operations Agent (Madeline) during World War II. She became the first female radio operator to be sent by the Allies into occupied France to aid the French Resistance (under General Charles de Gaulle). Captured by the Germans, Noor was executed in September 1944 when she was 30 and was posthumously given the highest civilian award (George Cross) by the British Govt in 1949. Recently, a special postage stamp was issued and a statue installed in her memory in Britain.

Dr A. Ali, who long ago organised lectures in Delhi by Pir Vilayat Khan on behalf of Hamdard, remembers him as a handsome man, with European features who had a mastery over written and spoken English and hardly looked like an Indian Sufi divine. Incidentally, his half- brother was an American Yogi. The message he preached (like his father) was that one does not have to embrace Islam to become a Sufi. Hazrat Inayat Khan had defined Sufism as a religious philosophy of love, harmony and beauty for all. His dargah is not far from the one of Hazrat Nizamuddin. Situated in an 'elegant modern structure', it is quite unlike the usual conception of a dargah. Some call it the 'white man's dargah' as most of the visitors are foreigners, who stay in the rooms attached to it and attend cultural events hosted by Dr Fareeda of the West Indies.

There are many in Delhi and elsewhere who do not subscribe to Inayat Khan's philosophy but still visit the dargah on Fridays when the qawwalis are held. This is a departure from tradition as qawwalis are generally held on Thursdays at Sufi dargahs.

Hazrat Inayat Khan preceded Maharishi Mahesh Yogi and Osho Rajneesh in popularizing Eastern philosophy abroad (to which Pandit Ravi Shankar also made his contribution) and the Beatles and Mia Farrow were among the devotees who came to India. Some how Inayat Khan did not attract much attention in Delhi, known as the 'threshold of the 22 Khwajas' or saints.

Be that as it may, it cannot he denied that the Sufi pir's daughter played a role in countering the Nazi dream of world domination, after trying her hand as a writer of children's stories and a stint in Paris as an artist. Did Noor Inayat Khan visit Delhi? No one is sure as there is no record of it, but Khushwant Singh, while once commenting on her, thought it was quite likely she did. For this he citied a member of the nizami family of pirs who escorted a pretty westernised young woman to the shrine of Inayat Khan on a cold, bleak, afternoon. Asked for her name she said it reflected the Noor of the saint and disappeared with a wave of her hand.

If she was really Noor Inayat, then the incident could have taken place before the war broke, though it is more likely that she came as a teenager during her father's funeral. Those were the days when people came in ships via the Suez Canal, landed in Calcutta or Bombay and then made their way to Delhi by train. But imagine Noor Inayat arriving at Old Delhi Station, all by herself later, which in itself was a courageous act. It was of the likes of her that Jawaharlal Nehru said that such heroines gave the lie to the belief that Eastern women were not meant to lead but to be led. One thinks of this when one visits Inayat Khan's dargah on a wet Friday evening.

A Legendary Doc

Doc Holiday may have been a favourite with youngsters watching Western cowboy films over five decades ago, but long before that Delhi had its own bearded Doc whom few remember now.

There were no motorised vehicles in 1879 when Dr Hem Chandra Sen came all the way here in a bullock cart from Agra. Rich people travelled in palanquins, buggies or four-wheeled *landaus* and the poor in *ekkas* and carts. Women hardly showed their faces in public, they either wore burqas or *ghoonghats* and there was no electricity and piped water supply.

In this milieu Dr Sen became the first Indian allopathic doctor of Delhi. From dispensing medicines to those building the E.I. Railways' Agra-Delhi line, he started treating the local populace before whom women did not mind uncovering their heads and faces. Dr H.C. Sen was credited with 'miraculous healing powers', his day beginning at 4 am and ending late at night. Rich and poor alike were treated by him. Those who could not come to his chambers were visited by him, for which he used two sets of horse carriages—one for the morning and the other for the evening. He charged ₹2 (for the full treatment) from those whom he visited at home and nothing from patients who came to his clinic. He set up a pharmacy also as getting medicines from Calcutta took a lot of time. Later it became a separate unit known as H.C. Sen and Company.

In 1883 Dr Sen founder of the Imperial Medical Hall, set up the Imperial Medical Press and type-setting moulding unit adjacent to his clinic. It was afterwards run by his nephew A.T. Roy, and the latter's sons and grandsons as one of the leading presses of Delhi. Member of the first management committee of Hindu College, Dr Sen played a leading role in youth education along with Lala

Shri Krishna Dass Gurwala (one of the founders of the college), M.M. Malaviya and many others of note.

Lala Krishan Dass Gurwala was among the seths who persuaded Dr Sen to settle down in Delhi. It is interesting to note that the name Gurwala was appended to the family as it used to provide *gur* and gram to pilgrims, says the centenary brochure on Dr Sen brought out in 1980. Gurwala's grandfather was hanged by the British for supporting Bahadur Shah Zafar. The family traces its history to 1560 and Lala Nodhamal of Akbar's reign. After Gurwala helped to establish the Delhi Cloth and General Mills, it meant an extended practice for Dr Sen.

However, when the good doctor fell seriously ill due to his exertions ('grace under pressure', to quote Hemingway), the British Chief Commissioner of Delhi ensured that there was complete silence in the Fountain area of Chandni Chowk so that he was not disturbed. It's worth mentioning that when Unani medicines were ineffective even the famous Ballimaran *hakims* did not hesitate in referring patients to Dr Sen for a speedier cure.

Europeans also came to Dr Sen, a Freemason, for treatment and for advice even on personal matters. Born in Calcutta before the 1857 Revolt, he died in 1906 and the Delhi markets were closed for a week as a mark of respect. He was succeeded by his sons, Dr B.C. Sen and Dr R.B. Sen (Adu Babu). From 1880 till his death Dr Sen had stayed on in Delhi and among his guests were Rabindranath Tagore, Swami Vivekananda, novelist Sarat Chandra, Sir Surendranath Bannerji, Subas Chandra Bose, Madan Mohan Malaviya, Hakim Ajmal Khan and the Maharajas of Jaipur and Jodhpur. Interestingly, Vivekananda used to walk to the Yamuna every day through Chandni Chowk so long as he stayed in Delhi.

The road from the Fountain leading to Old Delhi station is named after Dr Sen and on Ansari Road in Daryaganj his descendants continue to maintain their 100-year-old pharmacy. Now a book on the legendary doctor, an initiator of Durga Puja in Delhi, is being written (at the behest of Anees Enterprises) by Shipra Sen to commemorate her ancestor whose medicines for curing diseases like jaundice, other liver infections and malaria are still popular. May be Doc Holiday too would have got rid of his bottle-induced problems had he cared to saunter (shoulder-strapped gun and all) into Dr Sen's celebrated 19th century *maktab* at the *phuwara*!

Reshma Sings No More

Reshma, the gypsy girl with the haunting voice, breathed her last at a hospital in Lahore one Diwali eve. She was (what an irony?) suffering from throat cancer and had undergone treatment abroad too, but to no avail. The chubby face had become a bony mask and her ever-bright eyes had sunk into their sockets. A sad end to a legendary singer. One remembers hearing her at Yashwant Place at a soiree held for music lovers by danseuse Pushpa Dogra, If one is not mistaken, Kuldip Nayar, Rais Mirza and the late music critic Jitendra Pratap were among them. Reshma's child was suffering from dehydration and she had to leave from time to time to attend to him but that did not mar the recital.

It was a half-moon night and somebody whispered that Raj Kapoor had already heard the singer and, charmed by her voice, had signed her for his film, but when asked for the amount she would charge, she had replied something to the effect that singing for a film by a Bollywood idol was in itself a big honour. It showed the naivety of one who had started singing under the name of Reshma Banjaran.

Like Mehtab of Sindh, of the pre-Mutiny times, who was called the Donna of Larkhana, she charmed General Yahya Khan, fond of wine parties, music and dancing and from that time thereon earned a name for herself. Her's were not the warbled Persian songs of Alfina of the early 18th century, nor the passionate ones of Rehema Bibi or Zebunissa, but more in keeping with the locale of the Thar desert, verging on the *Sufiana kalaam* of Allan Fakir (who also came to charm Delhi).

She did not know it, but chroniclers like Pran Nevile thought her to be a second Mehtab come to life. On hearing the crooning gypsy girls of today, who come to the Saturday market and sometimes break into a song for lack of customers for the wares they sell, one is reminded of Reshma and of Husna, who lived and died long before her.

Husna was neither a dancer nor a beautiful *pari*. She was a poor beggar, much like the blind girl, Nydia, who sang and sold flowers in Pompeii—even on the afternoon of the fateful day in AD 79 when lava from Mount Vesuvius buried the city and its inhabitants.

Blind girls and boys do normally sing well. Husna's is a hearsay story, made romantic by the halo of time. But one remembers a girl who used to sell flowers in Connaught Place in the early 1960s. She was a wisp of a girl, offering *gajra* for the hairdo in front of cinema houses. But her voice, which was shrill in the beginning, became sweeter with maturity, and that was her undoing too, because Bela, began to be exploited by the lecherous who roamed the streets. She used to live in a *jhuggi* and came out in the evening, staying on till the wee hours. But gradually, she started performing the vanishing trick, until finally one missed her altogether. That was the end of Bela as far as the frequenters of Connaught Place were concerned.

Then one heard Chameli, a gypsy girl of Gauadia Lohars, sing in Jhandewalan. What a voice she had! One fell in love with it as soon as she opened her mouth. But someone who met her ten years later was taken aback by her appearance and voice. A boy from Paharganj had seduced her and after motherhood her talent was gone.

Reshma too was of the same tribe, even though she was brought up in Pakistan. But then the gypsies do not go by geographical limits. Their stage is the world, and you will find them adhering to their traditions wherever they are. Reshma sang the song of mankind which Wordsworth so eloquently described as the 'still sad music of humanity'. Her voice had an earthy fragrance that charmed the listener by its sincerity. As she sat on the glittering stage before a sophisticated audience, one had just to close one's eyes to transport the occasion to a desert scene—the cool night, with the moon shining on the dreary wastes and a caravan of camels on its perennial journey. Suddenly, the silence is broken by a silvery voice that offsets the tedium of the journey. The camels swing on their long legs and their riders with them, but the song goes on (remember how I.S. Johar fell down from one of them in the megafilm *Lawrence of Arabia* but was lucky to be picked up before the murderous sun came out). In the urbane Delhi setting where Reshma sang, one was reminded of such a scene, for despite her flabby exterior Reshma's was still the voice of a girl singing below the stars and enchanting the listener by the resultant melody that emerged—neither soft nor harsh, but overflowing with the milk of human pathos. No wonder not a few men and women were found swooning because the evening's magic had transported them to a world where melody was supreme. One hopes this tradition continues and that, after Reshma, gypsy girls do not disappear in the maelstrom of modernism. Reshma survived for 66 years, why can not the others of her tribe be able to do so too? But her *Lambi Judai* will be difficult to bear, *Ya Rabba*!

Of Melody, Nuance and Compère

Among those who graced Delhi's cultural scene 30 years ago was Rais Mirza, compère par excellence at mushairas, social singing contests, cultural performances and qawwali recitations. His wife Taramani was head of the Khadi Gram Udyog Bhavan in Connaught Place and they lived in Sriniwaspuri. That was the time when Charles Fabri, the Austrian art, drama, music and architecture expert, domiciled in India after an invitation from Rabindranath Tagore, had left Shantiniketan and settled down in Delhi with his wife Ratna Mathur, an interior designer of note, and their cute son Christopher. He was an art critic for the *Statesman*, whose Hindustani drama critic was Habib Tanveer, assisted by T.P. Jain. The latter went on to join Bollywood where he made a name for himself with his elfin face as a character actor. One used to meet 'T.P.' at Prantha Gali, where he lived and came out to drink an after-dinner *kulhar* of milk, over which he discussed the plays he had acted in or reviewed.

However, whenever one met Rais Mirza, dressed in a sherwani and pyjamas, with a tilted cap on his head, one felt as though a dacadent Lucknow litterateur had somehow been transported to the 20th century. There were many occasions when he excelled in compèring but the most memorable perhaps was the one about a performance of Habib Painter, the near-legendary *qawwal*.

Habib, born in 1915, had begun life as a billboard painter at Aligarh, much like M.F. Husain in Indore. His golden voice attracted a music lover whose patronage helped him to attain national status.

He came to Delhi often with his troupe and earned great acclaim. Well at the function alluded to, Rais Mirza sat on one side on the stage as Habib Painter rendered his *Sufiana kalaam* and then reverted to some popular numbers, including one of village belles drawing water for their homes. In his nasal tone he made the audience tipsy as he sang the lines about the difficult access to the well (*Badi kathin hai dagar panghat ki*) which, after a pause, Rais Mirza explained as a unique heel-toe-and-hip-straining experience, denied to women of other countries, trying to fill pots and pails, in times when piped water supply was not even a dream.

There are many *qawwal*s but Habib was different in that whatever he sang pulsated with nerve-tingling imagery. His love of music brought him into the limelight, especially during the Chinese invasion in 1962 when he sang for the troops. His efforts did not go unrecognised, for he was honoured with the award of Bulbul-i-Hind by Jawaharlal Nehru.

Habib was a simple man who combined Hindu and Muslim culture to bring home the message of integration. He did not sing only of the Kaba, the Koh-Qaf and the bulbul, but also of the child Krishna breaking the *chatties* of the gopis on the hillocks of Vrindavan. He sang for 50 years, and many of his accompanists became old with him because they preferred his company rather than the glamour of filmdom. Of them Rafiq Ali went on to earn much kudos.

At a cultural programme in Delhi, Habib entertained the assembly with a qawwali based on the mythical belief of how Tvashtri created woman:

> He took the lightness of the leaf and the glance of the fawn, the gaiety of the sun's rays and the tears of the mist; the inconsistency of the wind and the timidity of the hare; the vanity of the peacock and the softness of the dawn on the throat of the swallow. He added the harshness of the diamond, the sweet flavour of honey, the cruelty of the tiger, the warmth of the fire, and the chill of the snow. He also included the chatter of the jay and the cooing of the dove, and lo, the first female came into being...

But to come back to that long-lost evening, one was bemused to see Fabri, wearing his trademark three-piece suit and felt hat, complimenting the ladies, bowing to them and kissing their hands while the Rev J.D. Tytler (adoptive father of a political leader) audibly whispered, 'Will someone stop the lech?' That was during a break when Rais Bhai had a sip of water, Habib wiped the perspiration from his face and film critic Amita Malik got busy with her vanity case. Afterwards Habib Painter left for a tour of East Africa, courtesy actress Mumtaz, but felt homesick and returned to his beloved Aligarh where he expired on 22 February 1987, aged 72 and was buried in a mud grave.

The Falcon-Fanciers

The *shikra* (falcon) of Saeed Ahmad, an Indo-Turk, is now part of memory. The falcon would sit on his wrist and at a pull of its string would shoot up and catch a small bird, usually a sparrow or a shyama. It was fed read meat and feared by children who were wary of its sudden snap at their fingers. Saeed used to wear a leather band on his wrist to protect it from the impulsive bird of prey. Those were the days when some of the rajas and nawabs flaunted falcons like people do mobiles these days. Nagaland is famous for falcons migrating from colder climes in winter, coming to roost every year during their flight from Eastern Russia and China to Somalia, Kenya and South Africa. Thousands of them had been massacred by the Nagas over the years for consumption, but now conservation efforts have stopped it.

Falconry is thousands of years old. It was known in India as early as the Mahabharata days. The Egyptians, Greeks and Romans, as also the Chinese and Japanese, were fond of falconry. A falcon of Duryodhan snatched an ornament of Daraupdi and was shot and injured by one of the Pandavas-something that the Kaurava leader resented very much until calmed down by his machiavellian uncle, Shakuni. The falcon of Bhishma Pitamaha is a favourite part of local lore but does not form part of the Mahabharata epic.

Babar and Humayun's love for falcons was passed on to Akbar, who had them in his private quarters in the Agra Fort.

But when the emperor's prized pigeons were killed by them one night he had them caged so that his birds were kept out of harm's way. Jahangir spotted a *shikra* in his youth at Fatehpur Sikri and Shahjahan as Khurram had one presented to him by a Rajput prince with whom he and Mumtaz Mahal had taken shelter during his revolt against his father. A falcon was Guru Govind Singh's favourite bird.

In our own times Saeed Ahmad's *shikra* led to a craze for falcons in the Walled City. The nawabs of Basai Darapur (Delhi) and Jhajjar (Haryana) were known falconers, so also Nawab Shamsuddin Khan of Firozepur, who was hanged for the assassination of the British Resident William Fraser. The latter's friend, Col James Skinner saw a *shikra* aiding the Marathas during a battle. It belonged to Luckwa Dada, a crafty general of the Scindias.

The Colonel, a great hunter, acquired one for himself and in later years he would travel with it from his estate in Hansi to his mansion in Kashmere Gate. However, Colonel Ochterlony, who defended Delhi against Jaswant Rao Holkar in 1804, is said to have had a dislike for falcons. Some said a falcon of Holkar's had plucked out an eye of one of his soldiers guarding the city wall between the Delhi and Ajmeri gates.

During the Revolt of 1857, Maj-Gen John Nicholson too had his falcon when he laid siege to Delhi. What happened to it following the General's death, after being fatally shot at Lahori Gate, is not known. One heard these stories from Mian Sahib, a wizened old man who used to come for his evening meals to Hafiz Hotel in Ballimaran. He would talk nineteen to the dozen while eating dinner and after he left, the hotel owner would shake his head and say, 'God knows how much of what he says is true and how much is just gossip picked up on the roadside.'

The falcon was also a bird of omen. On seeing it Indira Gandhi was fatally shot by her guards in 1984. Saeed Ahmad's *shikra* just flew away one day and was never seen again. However, Mian Sahib's tale of the Mir Sahib, who had a lock of hair of his *purdah-nashin* beloved plucked by a pet falcon, is to be taken with a pinch of salt.

Puppet and Puppeteer

The Kathputli colony, which bears a striking resemblance to Kathpotli town on the way to Jaipur, came into being in the 1950s when the longest route, bus No. 9, from Kingsway Camp used to end in the vicinity at Shadipur after its extension from the original end-point, Reading Road (now Mandir Marg).

It is worth recalling that the ground occupied by the colony was once part of the Chauhan Rajput (1180–1192) stronghold as it was there that the remnants of Prithviraj's clan had holed up during the initial years of the Delhi Sultanate following Rai Pithora's defeat in the Second Battle of Tarain (1192).

In those days there was no Karol Bagh but the area beyond the Jhandewalan temple was protected by the Ridge, which served as a barrier to the expansion of the Sultanate.

When the nomads from Rajasthan occupied the vacant land that was to become their colony some 60 years ago it was not as if they were trying to reclaim the places associated with the Chauhan Rajputs, who ruled from both Delhi and Ajmer. The reason was that there was no hindrance to their camping there as it was outside the city limits. However, one attraction was that trains to Jaipur and other Rajasthan cities passed that way and fed the nostalgia for their erstwhile habitation.

One remembers cycling to the colony, not known as Kathputli then, from Regharpura, where the Reghars or dealers in skins engaged in shoe making, had settled down. The Reghars were the camp followers of armies engaged in internecine battles during the twilight of the Mughals, though some think, even earlier. After the battle they would skin the carcasses of animals and also allegedly plunder whatever they could. The Reghars like the residents of Kathputli colony, also had a Rajasthani link.

The puppets were not all Dhola-Maru and the 'blind camel' stuff. There were those of Rajput rajas and chieftains like Alaha and Udhal, also those of Pathan and Mughal rulers and of Anarkali and Salim; comic characters in the form of the 'Dhobi and Dhoban' and the 'Tees Mar Khan' (who killed 30 flies and gained the hand of the king's daughter as her father thought that he had slain 30 warriors). A touching scene was of the washerwoman weeping for her husband, carried away by a crocodile.

At dusk the puppeteer arrived with his wife and child, still not weaned, and set up a cot covered with a sheet, placed a lantern in front of it and the *tamasha* began, with the audience seated all around and the wife playing the *dholak*, while her husband played the flute or *tateeri*, besides juggling the puppets. One of whom kept up the refrain: *Thodi, thodi aur bajeygi* (I'll play a bit more).

The most popular puppet was Amar Singh Rathore, who had defied the might of Shahjahan at the royal court by slaying Salabat Khan, Nur Jahan's kinsman though he lost his life too, along with that of the horse on which he had jumped over the walls of the Agra Fort.

There was a comely daughter of a puppeteer who was much sought after by young men of her tribe with a roving eye. She eloped with one of them but he ditched her and so also two others after him. Eventually, she married an elderly man and had children but lost her beauty for which she had become famous.

The Yarn-Spinners

Nazir Mian was a storyteller. The opium addict with rheumed eyes, sat on the southern steps of the Jama Masjid and woke up as though from a trance when someone called him by name. No one ever saw him eating. Morning, noon and night he took out a little tin box from his soiled kurta pocket and put something in his mouth that looked like wet supari (betel nut). It was actually opium which brought him back to life or so it seemed. Once thus aroused, he would start entertaining a group of men, either retired or off-duty shopkeepers, with stories. He reminded one of the. Dastangos, the 16th-century Urdu oral storytellers, who lived and passed away in anonymity.

His favourite one was about Anar-di badshahzadi (Pomegranate Princess), who had been turned into a pomegranate by her wicked stepmother. One day a prince who was passing by broke the treasured pomegranate in the royal garden and ended the spell. The princess reassumed her beauteous form and married the handsome prince. The king only then came to know about the witch who had become his second queen and banished her from his kingdom. 'The young couple lived happily ever after', concluded Nazir Mian, trying to open his eyes wide and getting some money from the hearers, which he spent in buying opium from the licenced Govt shop in D.B. Gupta Road.

That was about one local storyteller. Among the well-known international ones were such greats as R.L. Stevenson, Somerset Maugham and Ernest Hemingway. When as a child Stevenson was punished and asked to stand in a dark corner at night, he shrugged off his nurse's attempts to keep him from getting frightened, by blurting out, 'Shut up ma'am, I'm telling myself a story'. Maugham claimed in later life that he could spin a yarn about nearly every one he met on the street. Hemingway's stories about the fisherfolk on the sea shore still strike a deep chord in the heart, something that the Bard of Avon did with superb felicity. The same thing was manifest in the parables of Christ, like *The Good Samaritan*, *The Prodigal Son* and *Dives and Lazarus*.

Nearer home there was Asghar Sahib, who related Mutiny yarns while Salim Pehalwan, who sat under the peepul tree at Delhi Gate, stopped passers-by to tell a tale which sent them home with their ears buzzing. It was an almost incoherent recital of something that happened in the 1940s, when he fell in love with a *kothawali* (sex worker), who in turn was fascinated by his manhood. Then came a day when Salim lost all the money he had earned while working at the nawab's and was kicked out from the *kotha*. It made him lose his mental balance and he always ended his story by pointing to a tin lying under the peepul, '*Da se dibba, dar he dar hai*' (That dibba or empty tin denotes fear and only fear).

Lame Rasool was invariably found at Hare Bhare's mazar and drew a crowd every afternoon, telling tales like that of Dildar Khan, a eunuch who was a chamberlain in the Red Fort and had fallen in love with a girl residing near his house in Chawri Bazaar. One night they were found in a compromising position on the roof of the girl's house by her brother, who slew both with a sword. They say the two still wander about during moonlit nights. Rasool's tales brought him enough to buy lunch and dinner too at Gharib Hotel.

Dastangos, like Mir Baqar Ali of Ballimaran, have passed into legend but not so Mianji of Azad Park's Kalimullah shrine. Mianji's tale was about how he went on a Hawai Haj (flying not in a plane but on the shoulders of a Jinn) while the wife thought he was fast asleep for three days. Many aspiring Hajis were among those who flocked to hear him, for his description of Mecca and Medina was absolutely true, something amazing for someone who had ostensibly never been out of Delhi.

Among the modern storytellers, Vijay Shankar is very impressive. One of his stories is about a Khan Sahib, who lived in arrears at a hotel in Jama Masjid's fish market, away from his family. When lucky he supplied liquor to Delhi's embassies on a commission basis. Fond of the stuff himself, Khan Sahib often shared a bottle with his companions, who then had to stand him dinner at Karim's. One night he saw a girl under a lamppost. Amorous as he was, despite his age, he hurried to her, thinking he had found someone to warm his lonely bed. But when he saw her face, he turned away in disgust. It was his daughter who, unknown to him, had become a streetwalker to help run the household. That's how true tales end and it's for the storyteller to bring out the pathos.

Anecdotes and Blindman's Tale

Like blindman Pew in R.L. Stevenson's *Treasure Island*, Krishna Sahai, a thick-set man, tapped his way with a walking stick, reciting couplets of Nazeer Akbarabadi or Surdas' dohas, to Dr Saksena's clinic in, predominantly, Muslim Panni Gali every evening.

Dr Saksena was the head of the department of skin and allied diseases at a government hospital but between 6 and 9 pm he practiced as a GP, with burqa women, prominent among the patients, like that of Dr Prem Behari Mathur, near the fountain in Chandni Chowk, a polular hereditary medical practitioner.

Krishan Sahai would sit quietly on a chair staring vacantly, at the side of the good doctor—whose childhood friend he had been since he lost his sight—and left only when the charitable dispensary closed.

However, there were times when patients were few or far between, like on cold or rainy days, and it was then that Sahai would speak to while away the time, followed by some historical anecdote by the doctor, prefaced with the observation that not all the *kahishtas* who had followed Shahjahan to Delhi, stayed on. They as a caste generally served as literary aides and munshis during Mughal days as they had a good knowledge of Urdu and Russian. Some went back to Agra, among whom was his great-great grandfather, who preferred the galis of his birthplace to those of the newly-built Shahjehanabad.

One story Dr Saksena never tired of relating was about the first western-type dispensary set up in Ballimaran by Dr Balfour, who had been the Civil Surgeon of the Civil Hospital before 1857.

This hospital was situated in the vicinity of the Red Fort, near a tank called the Laldigi. However, it had only eight indoor patients, leaving enough time for Dr Balfour, an adventurous Scotsman, and younger contemporary of Sir Walter Scott to revise his professional notes (like Sherlock Holmes' creator Arthur Conan Doyle) made in far-away Edinburgh, where he also learnt to fence, box and hunt deer in the Highlands. When the Great Revolt broke out in Delhi, Dr Balfour managed to escape, but his assistant, Dr Chimman Lal, a Christian convert, was among the first to be killed.

Dr Balfour found refuge in Kailana, where he was given protection by the *lambardar* of that village. It was on his return that Dr Balfour set up the Ballimaran dispensary which functioned for three years under the charge of an Indian doctor (before the new Civil Hospital was completed by Dr Smith in 1861), with 28 men and six women as indoor patients—among whom were two princesses and three maids of honour. The operations were, however, performed in a house rented by the civil surgeon, which was situated in better hygienic surroundings and also served as the outpatients' department with native and Anglo-Indian nurses (one of whom eloped with a pauper Mughal prince).

Another story heard from Dr Saksena was about Mitra Sen, whose samadhi is situated in Mitraon village, west of Najafgarh. According to Indian National Trust for Art and Cultural Heritage (INTACH):

> The samadhi is a very striking building, and the only one of its kind in Delhi. It has a central square chamber and a verandha

running all around it. Over the chamber stands a domed octagonal chattri or canopy.

But who was Mitra Sen? Not just another Sen but a powerful chieftain with a private militia, in the aftermath of Aurangzeb's death. Dr Saksena quoted from an old gazetteer to throw light on him.

> Jahandar Shah took over as Mughal emperor after the death of Bahadur Shah I and got most of the other claimants killed. Among those who escaped was his nephew Farrukhsiyar who, with the help of the Sayyid Brothers, defeated Jahandar Shah and executed him in 1712. Seven years later Farrukhsiyar's reign too ended when he was murdered in the Red Fort. Rafi-ud-darajat, Bahadur Shah's grandson, was then put on the throne by the Sayyids but the rebel garrison of Agra brought Nekusiyar, grandson of Aurangzeb, out of prison and proclaimed him emperor. The leader of this garrison was Mitra Sen. However, the new ruler died soon after and his elder brother ascended the throne as Shahjahan II for three months.

In the meantime—added Krishan Sahai—the Sayyid Brothers seized the treasure in the Agra Fort, the property of Nur Jahan and Mumtaz Mahal, as also the pall of pearls laid on the tomb of the empress in the Taj on Friday nights and the anniversary of her marriage.

After the death of Shahjahan II—resumed Dr Saksena—Mohammad Roshan Akhtar, son of Jahandar Shah, was crowned king by the Sayyids and began to rule as Mohammad Rangila. Mitra Sen managed to win the new ruler's favour and retired to a remote area of Delhi where he founded Mitraon village and where he continued to live until his death.

Dr Saksena is long dead and so also his friend Krishan Sahai, but some still remember him as the noted skin specialist who, because of his wide girth, preferred to sit and unravel medieval anecdotes like what caused the death of Bibi Akbarabadi of Shalimar Bagh fame rather than spend the morning exercising in the erstwhile Hewett Park.

World War Reminiscences

World War II days often come to mind and do not seem so distant to old-timers. There was Uncle James, Chunu Chacha to the kids, who would go up the narrow staircase of his 1869 house and, putting his hand slyly up the opening in the tin canopy, deftly catch a pariah kite. He would bring it down, tie a piece of paper to its leg with the words; 'Hitler the Great/was born in a plate/in the year 1938' and release the bird, which would fly away into the trees in the adjacent nawab sahib's *kothi* in Old Delhi much to every one's amusement. Probably his dexterity helped him to avoid getting pecked.

Those were the days of civil defence drills. Silent war movies were shown and red poppies distributed in November (on contribution basis) to mark World War I. The Taj Mahal's dome was camouflaged with a scaffolding so that the German jerry could not drop a bomb over it or so it was believed. When evening came there was a blackout and children doing their homework had to sit with a lantern around whose chimney brown paper had been wound so that the light could not be seen from a plane.

That was also the time when Chirront, a short, comical, sparrow-faced boy used to come in, followed by Indo-Turk brothers Iqbal and Mehfooz who pulled his leg as he used to think that the daughter of his landlady, at Ishrat Manzil, had been locked in a room to prevent him from meeting her. Chirront, whose real name was Arshad Husain, later began styling himself as 'Rev. Kennedy' and his idiosyncrasies nearly led to the arrest of his father as he told the police that the old man was a Nazi informer.

The afternoons of the early 1940s saw a man coming on a bicycle to distribute British emblem flags and war pamphlets with pictures of wounded soldiers and Red Cross nurses. Also depictions of bombed sites in Europe, Africa and the Far East, where the Japanese were fighting against the Allies. Anglo-Indian nurses were in great demand and among them was Dulcie Alexander, smoking a slim cigarette when she came on leave to visit her family. The locality boys used to think the 'Lal Bibi' was a foreign actress in skirt and blouse with bobbed hair, long legs and high-heeled shoes, come to entertain the American soldiers staying in the barracks opposite Delhi station. The Italian priests, including Father Luke, builder of Sacred Heart Cathedral, were interned near the Italian POW camp in Dehradun from where one prisoner, Multedo later married Dulcie's younger sister, Eena. Incidentally, those guarding the POWs included Jim Corbett and fellow-shikari Cyril Thomas.

Every day the papers were full of War news and cartoons by Ahmed, one of which showed Hitler and Mussolini as two bald vultures sitting on a withered tree with a nest containing an egg-shaped bomb. Ahmed later migrated to Karachi but was greatly missed by newspaper readers who were constantly informed that after the ouster of Rommel, the Desert Fox, and the flight of Rudolf Hess to Britain that the War was soon going to end. That was cheering news for the Walled City, facing acute shortage of the rationed safety matches, candles, salt, sugar and kerosene. Army canteens, however, were popular for supplying (at concessional rates) milk and egg powder as also tins of butteroil. The skies were illuminated with searchlights at night and during the day flew planes connected to their carriers with iron chains, making an old woman think her son was knotting them as part of his job at the Cantonment Ordnance Depot.

When the War ended big parades were taken out all over the country and 'V' for victory signs set up. Delhi witnessed a grand parade too (a precursor to our own R-Day parade?). Besides the troops marching in formation, there were open trucks showing men cutting trees, dismantling bombs and nurses treating the injured. Tanks also formed part of the parade, followed by weapon-carriers seated in which tanned Tommies with dishevelled hair gave dirty looks, provoking some to remark that they were the Hoosh (frenzied Firangis) eyeing local girls after being cut off from their '*mems*' for long.

Those times are past. Chunu Chacha is long dead and the trees in the nawab's *kothi* have been cut down to make room for a school that has come up there after the death of all, but one member of the family. Choti bubu now lives as an octogenarian in Sindh. But the War Arch at India Gate, the museum in the Red Fort, the cemetery at Brar Square and recurring anniversaries are still vivid reminders of the two World Wars.

Poesy on Tombstones

James Cummins was a Telegraph master in Delhi who died after he was struck by lightning in the 19th century. He is buried in the cemetery named after General Nicholson and his tombstone says:

> Left behind a wife and child bewailing his loss.

If one wanders further one comes across this epitaph:

> Passing Stranger call this not/A place of dreary gloom/
> I love to linger near this spot/It is my beloved mother's tomb.

Just at the entrance of the cemetery is a small marble tablet mourning a six-month-old child whose death had devastated its parents. Nicholson, who lies buried nearby, has been eulogised both in English and Urdu.

In the St. James' churchyard are buried the wife and five daughters of George Beresford, Manager of the Delhi Bank, who were killed on 11 May 1857, in Chandni Chowk. The rebel sepoys had attacked the bank building and though Beresford put up a stout resistance, it was his wife who proved more heroic, killing two of her attackers with a seized spear before falling down fatally injured.

In Lothian Road Cemetery is the grave of a merchant who married four times and

> Buried three wives, but the fourth did for him!

There are some pithy epitaphs in the Paharganj, Prithviraj Road and Rajpur Road cemeteries too. In Paharganj is a tomb which was in the news some time ago as it vibrated for five minutes when the priest blessed it on All Souls' Day. There is, or used to be, one tombstone that had the words 'Damn You' written on it. Whether it was meant to damn the visitor or the ones who had buried the person is not known.

The oldest British-time tombs are, of course, in Kolkata, including that of Rose Alymer, who died young and on whom Walter Savage Landor (1775–1864), wrote these lines:

> Ah, what avails the sceptred race!
> Ah, what the form divine!
> What every virtue, every grace! Rosy Aylmer, all were thine.

Some of the epitaphs in Delhi are about just as old and no less memorable because of the poetic strain in them. The new graves in Burhari and Dwarka, however, are mud ones with no epitaphs.

According to E.A.H. Blunt, ICS, writing in 1911, the old epitaphs were not without some unconscious humour, like a man who died

> Craving a large widow and family to mourn his loss.

Another one proclaims:

> Good attendance was applied, Physicians were in vain.

Blunt goes on to say, 'If pigmies must squabble about a dead giant, they should at least have the decency not to do so over a giant's grave' (This was said in connection with a hero of 1857). Incidentally, an unlikely hero was 'a gallant French circus master who went out to fight with Anglo-Indian volunteers that year for the 'honour of the alliance'. Capt. (later Lt-Col) W. R. Pogan, author of the *History of the Bundelas* (1787–1843), was noted for both his learning and eccentricity. As per his wish, he was buried on a roadside within sound of bugles' (on the far side of the infantry parade ground) where young buglers came for practice every day.

Colonel Skinner, who is buried in the church built by him at Kashmere Gate, has this epitaph:

> Here rest the remains of the late Colonel James Skinner G.B. who departed this life at Hansi, 4th December 1841.
>
> The body was disinterred, removed from Hansi and buried under this on the 19th January 1842.

Sixty-three gun salutes were fired, 'denoting the number of years of the deceased'. It was further stated that 'none of the emperors was ever brought into Delhee is such state as Secunder Sahib' (as he was known). Earlier, the Colonel had a beautiful marble tomb constructed for William Fraser, assassinated British Resident, with this tribute:

> So you see by the blessing of God, I have served Him and my friend too, whose memory and love remain firm in my old heart. In him I have lost the best friend I had in the world...and my friendship with the world ends with him.

More poignant is this Urdu epitaph on a young wife:

> *Na aiye raas chaman ko/Woh naubahar hoon main/*
> *Kisi ke aish do-roza/ki yaadgar hoon main*
> (I'm the blossom which did not suit the garden, a reminder of someone's two days of happiness)

The muse similarly wept for Justin Offley, an indigo merchant, killed in a Holi riot in 1637.